HOW CAN I BELIEVE
WHEN I LIVE
IN A WORLD LIKE THIS?

HOW CAN I BELIEVE
WHEN I LIVE
IN A WORLD LIKE THIS?

DR. REGINALD STACKHOUSE

HarperSanFrancisco
A Division of HarperCollins*Publishers*

First published 1990
by HarperCollinsPublishers

Copyright © 1990 Reginald Stackhouse

First Edition

ISBN 0-06-067512-8
LC 90-55302

To the memory of my parents

Who believed when they lived in a world like this

Table of Contents

CHAPTER ONE

Why is This Happening to Me?

"Why is this happening to me?" If you haven't yet asked yourself that question, be patient. You will.

Life has so many inexplicably cruel ways of challenging your assumptions, just as you convince yourself this world is a good place to live.

You may think you're on your way to realizing all your dreams when suddenly the roof falls in on you. One Friday afternoon the boss drops into your office, but not for a chat. He tells you you're being let go. Clean your desk out, he says, and don't come back on Monday. There's nothing wrong with your work. It's just a matter of the company being restructured. On your way home you try to figure it out. But you can't. All you can do is ask yourself, "Why is this happening to me?"

Or you walk out of a courtroom wondering how

you kept yourself under control. The drunk driver who killed your twelve-year-old daughter was given a fine and had his licence suspended for a year. You see him laughing with his wife and friends in the corridor and you wonder what your sentence would be if you killed him on the spot. On your way home you ask your husband: "What kind of a world is this? She's dead and he's laughing!"

Or it may be a natural catastrophe that makes you throw your hands up in despair. The TV news tells you that an earthquake has just shaken your home town to its foundations. You rush to the telephone to get word about your parents, but the lines are jammed and it takes worry-filled hours to get through. When you do, you learn your mother is safe but your father is missing. Your mother tells you he may be in the rubble of the collapsed expressway on which he would have been driving home from work. "But that expressway's earthquake proof," you protest. "That's what we've always been told," is all she can comment, too numb with anxiety to argue. "What can a person believe anymore?" you ask yourself.

None of these examples is farfetched. Anyone of those could be a neighbor or an associate — or yourself. This world is not an easy place to live for anyone who thinks life should fit together. It can challenge anyone with a religious faith to ask: "How can a person go on believing in God when life does not show us somebody good and powerful is in charge?"

But it's a problem too for people without a religious faith. Relying on the human race to be motivated by an inherent rational goodness is just as difficult in a world like this as believing in God. We do not need much philosophical debate to see it. The TV news can show us any night of the week. A passenger plane is shot down because its pilot refuses an order to land when it flies over forbidden territory. A cruise ship is seized by terrorists who push a man in a wheelchair into the sea when they learn he is Jewish. A woman jogging in a city park is first robbed, then raped and finally clubbed to death by youths whose only explanation is that it was fun. "How can I believe in God?" is hard to answer in a world like this. But "How can I believe in people?" is just as hard.

The problem of evil and innocent suffering has haunted me all the years I have spent — as pastor, professor and politician — helping people in trouble. Let me tell you about two who can be examples for everyone else.

I met them soon after I became the rector of a city parish church and found myself seated in the living room of their genteel home trying to make conversation with the genteel lady of the house. It was a frustrating effort, because, polite as she was, she did not seem with me. I soon learned why. As soon as her husband, a dignified, quiet spoken, composed man, entered the room, she leaped to her feet to ask: "What did the doctor tell you? Is, is...?" Her voice trailed away before she could complete words too painful to utter. They were too painful for him as well. All he could do was nod his head. She fled from the room to sob in private.

Alone with me, he explained that his doctor had just received the results of tests he had been given. The report was the worst possible case. He had inoperable cancer, and no alternative to surgery being available then, the report was a death sentence. He almost knew the day he would die because he had been told to expect just two more months.

What do you say to someone when he tells you he will be dead in two months? Especially when he explains how the long-cherished plans of his wife and himself have just been blown away like chaff in the wind. He had just been retired. Their home was free and clear. Their children were grown up and on their own. After a lifetime of duty and labor they were looking forward to a few years of freedom and pleasure. If the world were as it should be that did not seem too much to hope for. But the two of us saw as we talked together that this world was not that kind of place. What was due was not always paid.

The wound was all the deeper because the couple had been steadfast Christians, as faithful to God as to each other. Why could God not be just as faithful to them? Why was he letting them break up like two pieces of china dropped on the floor? Those questions filled my mind and his as he shared his soul with me. If he had renounced his faith then and there I would have had to understand why. I knew I would not treat my children that way. Why was God treating his like that? Perhaps, I had to think, Archibald MacLeish was right when he wrote his play *JB* and mused:

> If God is God, he is not good.
> If God is good, he is not God.
> Take the even, take the odd.

In the years since, the question has not gone away: How can I believe when I live in a world like this? The lack of an answer has not come from a lack of searching. Anyone who wants to make the effort can find almost more scholarly discussion than can be digested. Through the centuries theologians and philosophers have wrestled with this problem. But not only has no one provided a wholly satisfying answer. Some have made the problem worse.

The Solutions
Have Been Part
of the Problem

The Greek philosopher Plato tried to explain evil away by calling it a nothing — that is, the absence of being. Centuries later, St. Augustine taught much the same thing. In his view, everything that exists is good because it was created by God. Evil is

the absence of that good. It results from deprivation or "blank spots" in creation.

Let's try an example. A child is born with no fin-
gers.The mother asks how this can happen in
God's world since God is good and loves her child.
The answer of St. Augustine is that her child's life
is a divine gift and the child's lack of fingers is a
deprivation of part of that gift. God did not cause
the absence of the fingers but only the good creation of the rest of the child's body.

But that does not stop the mother asking who or
what prevented her child having fingers. It does
not stop her wondering why God did not act to
save this child from such a cruel deprivation. She is
not satisfied with the theology she has been
offered. It does not answer the question that is tear-
ing her soul apart: "Why has this happened to my
child?" God, she has been taught to sing, has the
whole world in his hands. Why hasn't he given full
hands to this baby? She cannot hold her tears back
as she watches the infant try to suck an invisible
thumb, not knowing there will never be one there
to suck or later to use.

That is why so much theology and philosophy
fail us on this point. They want to defend God's
integrity instead of satisfying people's anguish.
They want to use terms like primary and secondary
causes. They act as though a mother should relax
when she learns that God, as the primary cause of
life, was too far removed from her baby's prenatal
development to be blamed for this malformation.

Gottfried Wilhelm Leibniz, at the end of the seventeenth century, thought in this way. A diplomat for his German prince by day and a philosopher by night, he wrestled with the problem enough to give it the name by which it is still known — theodicy. This term comes from two Greek words, *theos* meaning God, and *dike* meaning justice. Leibniz also gave people a way of fitting the evils of this world with the belief a good God created it.

Best remembered for saying we live in "the best of all possible worlds," Leibniz tried to show how this could be believed even when the world contains babies without fingers. Although many readers assumed he meant it was a perfect world, that was not his point at all. He did not mean it was the best world people could conceive, but the best possible one. For Leibniz a world without evil and innocent suffering was not a possibility. Living in this world must mean accepting its imperfections and making the best of them.

According to this German philosopher, anything finite was imperfect just because it was finite and therefore limited. Imperfection thus went with a finite world. But this imperfection, Leibniz claimed, was not just something people have to live with. It was also an asset. Just as light needed to be set off by darkness, one season contrasted with the other three, and a painting enhanced by a frame, so the good things of this world could be best appreciated because evil was found alongside them.

As an argument, Leibniz' theodicy was not bad,

but I wonder if he would have talked that way to a mother whose baby had just been born malformed. She would want to ask him why her child had been deprived when so many others had been born whole. Just let a detached philosopher try to tell her the child had to suffer that way so that people could appreciate what normal life was like. That has been the problem with so much academic discussion of this problem. It has been so preoccupied with checking and balancing ideas, it has forgotten the problem is about people, not propositions.

That was why Francois Marie Arouet, the eighteenth century thinker best known as Voltaire, turned 180 degrees away from Leibniz. He saw the problem in its human terms, especially when he felt the shock of a terrifying tragedy that shook the thinking of all Europe.

Why Did God Cause
the Earthquake?

At twenty minutes to ten on the morning of All Saints' Day, November 1, 1755, tremors shook Lisbon so violently that six minutes after they started, a thousand homes had been destroyed, fifteen thousand people had been killed and another fifteen thousand fatally injured.

In three hundred and sixty seconds, that earthquake shook not only the capitol of Portugal but the assumptions of an entire civilization's exaggerated confidence in the natural order. "How could this happen to innocent people?" Voltaire and agonized people all over Europe asked. Lacking the instant global communication of today, eighteenth century men and women were not aware that almost every day disaster strikes somewhere on this planet. It was the "Age of Reason" and the intelligentsia had convinced themselves that the world was an orderly place, governed by rational laws. They were not intellectually prepared for the system suddenly running amok like a crazy gorilla.

Opinion makers flailed about offering traditional answers, pathetically unaware they did not fit. Some explained the disaster as a divine judgment on sin. This might have been a plausible interpretation if destruction had come to every city in Europe. But why would God have singled Lisbon out?

This theory was rendered more absurd when it meant applying this harsh judgment to people kneeling at prayer in the thirty churches destroyed in the quake. Did those people deserve the roof literally to fall in on them? Would a good God really rain death down on frail old people and young children at church and allow cutthroats, con men and swindlers outside to go free?

The determination to explain the inexplicable became more absurd still when some linked the tragedy to religion. Some said God had damned Lisbon because it was Roman Catholic. But how did that fit with similar earthquakes in Protestant and Muslim cities about the same time? Could it mean that God was really against all religions!

Even worse was the argument of one social philosopher that the suffering could have been avoided if people had been living on farms and in villages instead of a big city. An early critic of the urbanization trend, this analyst's theorizing got carried away. But obviously not far enough. What his argument showed was that the intellectuals of Europe had a question without an answer.

So Voltaire wrote a now classic novel, *Candide*, to make that very point. Contrary to Leibniz, this was not the best of all possible worlds but a place of violence, treachery, and brutality in which the innocent suffer far more than the guilty. There is no making sense out of it and all one can do is get on with life in the best way one can find.

Candide is the name of the novel's anti-hero, who travels three continents having adventures and misadventures. Wherever there is trouble Candide seems to find it. Conflict, pillaging, and cheating are as much part of his experience as they are in a modern television film. All this, of course, is to show how this is not the best of all possible worlds and how it is filled with innocent suffering that cannot be justified.

Finally Candide finds a man who seems genuinely happy. He appears to have everything Candide has ever wanted, has roamed the world seeking, and had almost concluded could not be found. Yet this man has none of the things for which Candide had found so many ready to fight, betray, even murder to gain. What is his secret, Candide asks. The man reacts with surprise. He has no secret, he says. He has no theory about happiness. He just enjoys life. He is too busy making a living for his family to think about it.

Such is the book's message. This is not a perfect world. There is misery everywhere. But there's not much value in thinking about it. No matter how much we try, we will not discover why some suffer and others prosper. We should not "think" existence, but live it. The best we can do is to give up arguing about unanswerable questions and get on with living. We cannot remake the world by debating its imperfections. But we can find good somewhere. When we do, we should make the most of it.

Strong stuff. And practical. It may strike you as callous, indifferent and hard-nosed. But its message is inescapable. It had to be accepted by a young man whose wife was killed in an accident while away on an annual outing with some school friends. When it happened, he wanted me as his pastor to tell him why this beautiful, vivacious young woman should be taken from the husband and children who loved her. But he could not keep bombarding me with that question. He had to put himself together. He had to make a home for his two children. He had to get on with life.

And yet that is not all that can be said. Voltaire's message was good, but not good enough. It was not enough for that young woman's parents, to whom I also ministered. "Why did this happen to her?" was a question they could not let go that easily. They felt they had a right to an answer. They did not want to treat their daughter's death as meaningless. That would have meant they saw her life that way too.

So the problem stays with us. If it were just an academic one it might be dropped. But it is an existential one and is just as insistent now as it was for any of the theologians and philosophers who addressed it through the ages. When I pick up the Bible I can almost believe the writers are contemporaries. Their messages are about your existence and mine as they write about evil and innocent suffering endured by people then just as much as now.

"Why is this happening to me?" is thus a question that takes us back to that ancient Hebrew poet who wrote:

"My God, my God, why have you forsaken me?" (Psalm 22: 1)

It takes us back to the cross of Jesus when he gasped those same words (Luke 27:46). Both men then, like so many people now, knew they did not deserve what was happening to them. They knew it did not fit the God in whom they had put their trust. How could they believe when they lived in a world like this?

That is why I want to to take this question back

to the Bible. Theology and philosophy have not been able to cope with it. So let's see what the Bible can offer us. Contrary to what so many assume, it is not a book about theology or philosophy or even religion. Primarily it is a collection of books about people and their struggle to make the best life they could in this uncertain world. The reason this collection has endured all these centuries and translated into every language known to humanity is that it helps its readers cope with existence. Let's see what it can tell us about why unjust things happen to people who do not deserve them.

The Book
of Job

To sharpen our focus, let's take a look at just one book — Job. It is not a biography of a man who actually lived. It is a story about a person who could live any time, anywhere. That is why it has a message for you and me.

A book as ancient as Job is not irrelevant to understanding our personal tragedies. The timeless can never be outdated and the Book of Job speaks to our condition as it did three thousand years ago. It is a story of an innocent man who suffered evil of dramatic proportions, without knowing the smallest reason that could justify it.

Job is not an historical person but a literary character who represents suffering humanity in every age, and who exposes the futility of so many attempts to explain why such evil descends on people. It is as up-to-date as it is ancient because it is existential. Job shares with us a human nature that has not changed. His experience speaks to an everlasting present.

Like any drama, the book opens with an effort to provide a context so that the audience — the reader — can understand what follows. Let us think of a stage curtain rising on the land of Uz, located somewhere northeast of Israel. Here in a kind of scriptural "Dallas" lives a patriarchal land-baron, perhaps the original man who has everything, a beneficent "Big Daddy." He has a family of seven sons and three daughters. He owns seven thousand sheep, three thousand camels, five hundred yoke of oxen and five hundred donkeys. He employs so many servants the author does not bother to give us a number.

Job is not just a money-worshipping magnate. The book describes him as blameless and upright, a man who fears God and turns away from wrong. Job's piety is so great that he regularly makes burnt offerings to God just in case any of his sons has sinned and cursed God in his heart.

As the story opens, Job's life is idyllic. He has no inkling that he is like a Titanic on course to hit an iceberg. That berg is about to be sent Job's way by God and Satan. The reader should not be troubled by the entrance of Satan. He is not a cult figure, nor is he dressed in red tights with a spear-pointed tail and horns. He is a symbol of evil, a dramatic device to communicate the book's message.

Satan gate-crashes a meeting between God and his sons. He tells God how he has been roaming the earth. God asks if he has met Job. Satan sneers that he knows all about Job and can write Job's goodness off because it has been bought and paid for. Since Job has received so much from God, why would Job not serve him? If God took it all away, Satan scoffs, then Job would curse God to his face.

God is stung by the charge. Have his assumptions about Job been naive? Impossible! God explodes, angrily confident that his demonic challenger will be overwhelmed when Job is put to the test. He tells Satan that Job is now in his hands — but with one caveat. No harm is to come to Job himself.

Then the whole world of Job seems to collapse. His oxen and donkeys are stolen by rustlers who kill Job's men when they defend the livestock. And this is only for starters! Job's sheep are struck by lightning. His camels are run off by bandits. Then a tornado sweeps across the plains and collapses the family home on Job's children as they are feasting inside.

Job is now at the edge of the poverty line. He does not have even a roof over his head. His downfall is complete. The first round in this supernatural struggle seems to have gone to Satan. How can Job still believe when he lives in a world like this?

Yet believe he does. On hearing the news about

his house and his family, he gives a simple
testimony of faith:

> Naked came I from my mother's womb,
> And naked shall I return.
> The Lord gave and the Lord has taken away.
> Blessed be the name of the Lord. (Job 1:21 NKJ)

There was more to Job than Satan had thought.
God had been right after all. But Satan will not
admit defeat. Instead he takes the offensive. Job is
faithful, he argues, because he is still hale and
hearty. If he had to suffer personally then he would
surely curse God. It is a clever retort and it touches
a divine nerve. God's reply sounds almost like a
concession:

> He is in your hands, but spare his life. (Job 2:6)

Once more catastrophe crashes down on Job. He
is struck with loathsome sores from head to foot.
While desperately scratching himself, he must also
listen to a nagging wife who advises him to curse
God, die and get it over with. But Job remains
unmoved by either his marital or his physical
affliction. He asks his wife if they should not expect
to receive some evil from the God who had given
them so much good. No answer is given, and that
is the end of the wife's cameo appearance. Satan
also disappears from the drama, never to return.

But for Job the drama has only just begun. As he

sits amid the ashes of his life, he is visited by three friends who come to share his sorrows. The visit does not work out that way because Job's friends offer a message that is as comforting as salt in a wound.

But their dialogue with Job is what the book is all about — trying to justify belief in God by people who have to live in an evil world. For these three friends that is no problem. They are so convinced of their answer that they cannot grasp why Job asks his question, "Why is this happening to me?" For them there is no such thing as innocent suffering because only guilty people suffer. If Job is suffering he must be guilty. They do not know what wrong he has done. Job doesn't either. But guilty he must be, because he is suffering.

The friends of Job are the classical dogmatists who demand that existence be fitted into their presuppositions, instead of believing dogmas should be adapted to existence. But Job will have none of their theorizing. He does not buy the proposition that he must be guilty because he is suffering. Until he learns what evil deed he has committed, he is not going to admit guilt. Job will not adapt his life to a system. The system must be adapted to life — or be changed.

Job, instead of conforming and making a ritual confession, makes a demand that leads to the climax of the drama. He demands an encounter with God himself. He is sure that is the only way he can gain an answer to his problem of why he is suffering. He does not want to go to scripture or visions or tradition, or to any of the other sources of religious beliefs. He wants something existential that will involve him as a person encountering another person. Job is thus the first modern person, the first human being to demand he be the center of understanding for his own existence.

The book includes one more trial for Job. When the friends leave him in disgust, he is challenged by Elihu, a character who just appears, for no other reason than to provide a bridge to the great meeting that is to come. His appearance reveals to Job something about himself he has not yet seen. Elihu tells him that if he would just stop talking and stand still for a while he would learn what he has been missing. He would gain a sense of proportion about himself and his place in the universe. He would grasp how great God is in creation, whether in the cosmic majesty of the heavens or in the micro-marvel of a raindrop. Then Job could do what he has not done. He could humble himself before God and accept existence as he finds it, instead of protesting that it should fulfil his expectations.

Job is given no time to defend himself. He suddenly finds himself before the divine judge he has sought so long.

In keeping with one of the Bible's basic beliefs — that God cannot be seen — God enters the drama but does not appear. Job can hear his voice but not see his face. What a voice it is! It is like a whirlwind sweeping across plains and deserts, carrying all before it and laying low anything that stands in its way. What Job hears from this rushing, mighty wind can be summed up in two questions that strip Job of all the pretensions that have been part of him. They are:

Where were you, Job, when I created the world? and
Who are you to demand that I explain myself to you?

Job must now humble himself by ceasing to see himself as someone special. He must accept himself as one creature among many others. Who is he to challenge the Creator?

At last Job is confounded. Gone is the grand rhetoric he had used to assail his friends. He now has no reply at all. All he can do is confess that he had spoken all along without understanding. But now things are different. He has at last realized that he can understand existence only when he stands under it. Now Job is able to see himself as he is, and to appreciate that there is no reason why he should escape the kind of suffering that others have to bear too. Suffering, he now sees, is as much part of being human as being born.

With that the drama is over, except for a Hollywood kind of ending. So short that it leaves the reader breathless, this last chapter returns Job to the land of Uz, where he finds all his family and possessions have been restored many times over. Job lives to be one hundred and forty, and enjoys his descendants for four generations until "old and full of days," he dies in peace.

*The Theodicies
of Job*

The benefit we can take from reading Job is finding six theodicies in its pages, either explicitly or by implication.They are ways of comprehending how there can be evil and innocent suffering in a world created by a God believed to be all powerful and all merciful. The remainder of this book will focus on discussing each one, and with it the major personal crisis that it addresses. We will also see how these theodicies apply even when people who have abandoned belief in God still want to believe they live in a world that is more than a jungle.

We will see that none of these theodicies offers a total answer. Each one suits a certain set of circumstances and not others. We will also see that when we have studied them all, we will not know all the answers! Instead we will see there is a mystery about evil and innocent suffering that cannot be probed, only accepted. It is here that we will find how vital believing is to coping with an existence as unpredictable as the kind you and I have.

The first theodicy of Job is the belief that whatever comes our way is God's will. If that is the case we will have to ask what kind of God could allow the suffering so many people have to bear. But we will also see there is truth in this claim, and be forced to see that even if we could be God for a day we would not govern the world differently.

The second theodicy is the explanation that suffering is either a divine judgment on sin, or at least the consequences of our corruption and our mistakes. That will drive us to ask what kind of world this is, and to wonder how it can be a place where the innocent suffer and the guilty are rewarded.

Theodicy number three is the positive side of the problem. Job is not the same man at the end of the story as he was at the beginning. He has matured through suffering. So we will look at how evil and innocent suffering contribute to our growth as men and women. But in the face of what so many have to endure, we will have to wrestle with wondering if there could not be some better way of teaching us. Is excruciating pain the only way to learn what we should know?

Fourth is the theodicy of vicarious suffering. We all know of inspiring sacrifices that have made life better for others.But is it fair to expect one person to pay for everyone else?

Fifth, the Book of Job gives us a glimpse into the evolving belief in a future life that was developing among the people of ancient Israel. Job lets us see some hope that there is a world beyond this one. He gives us a glimpse into a possibility that profoundly alters the entire way we look at evil and innocent suffering in this world. Not a widely held belief today, this theodicy will nonetheless drive us as modern people to ask just how this world can possibly be enough to meet the needs of a fully human existence.

The final theodicy will take us beyond the other five. Just as Job was confounded by the whirlwind, so we will be stumped by the way this problem will end in mystery. When we reach the end of our road, we will find there is no "there," there. We will therefore have to ask if anyone has ever made it through the pain of existence so successfully that no questions remained unanswered. We will then then see how believing is always better than not believing, because instead of fabricating answers to an unanswerable question, believing helps people to cope with life in a world like this.

But like Job, we will discover the greatest benefit of this probing will be what it shows us about ourselves. Once we stop looking at the problem as though it were an external object, we will see how the real answer lies in what suffering tells us about ourselves. Our world will not be different, but we will be.

*Why Not
You?*

That is the insight that made all the difference to a friend of mine who, like Job and so many of us, had gone through life thinking he knew what it was all about. Then everything fell apart. His wife had a series of strokes that rendered her totally dependent on others, mostly on him. The business he had operated successfully for years suddenly found itself in a crisis because of international currency developments quite beyond his control. One of his children developed an alcohol problem and another suffered a marriage breakdown.

Until then everything had been so different. When they married, all his friends raved about his wife and through the years he had been told over and over how lucky he was to have her beside him. The perfect hostess, the charming conversationalist, the exemplary mother, she offered him everything. So did his family when they were growing up, and the neighbors often spoke of their life as an example of what a home should offer. He had never known a day when business had not offered more than enough income and a respected status in the community.

Then it terminated as though a curtain had been drawn on his life, shutting out the light. A churchgoer, he wondered how all this squared with his faith. He had never thought of God except as someone to whom you turned in trouble. But there was no way out of the troubles that were now afflicting him as though they were Job's boils. One morning while driving to the office he wondered how long he could keep the place open. He could contain his soul no longer. He burst out: "Lord, why me?"

He did not expect an answer because, churchgoer or not, he was not a deeply religious man and had never felt anything akin to the presence of God. But expecting an answer or not, he received one. It was not what some of us might have expected God to tell him. It certainly was not a theodicy. Instead it was another question. When my friend asked God, "Why me?" the answer was simply: "Why not you?"

Discouraging? Disappointing? Embittering? Not at all. My friend saw what Job saw. Suffering is part of human existence, and no amount of believing will take it away or even explain it. None of us should expect to be insulated from it, even if we live as examples of faith and purity.

But we can expect that believing will help us to cope with what we cannot escape.

CHAPTER TWO

If You Could Be God for a Day What Would You Do with a World Like This?

Some people are convinced God is the problem and not the solution. If God were doing what he should, they reason, this world would be different. When they see what innocent people have to endure, they wonder what kind of God he is to will or at least allow all this in a world he governs.

But ask yourself if that is as true as it seems. If you could be God for a day, what would you do differently? Would you change it so that the innocent would not suffer? You might find the cure was worse than the disease and not change things as much as you thought you would. Let me tell you about a real-life incident to show you what I mean.

The world seemed a good place to live that Saturday morning when I got up. My Sunday sermon was ready. I had nothing to do at the church until the afternoon. My wife and I began to think of ways we could enjoy the bonus of a free morning. Then the telephone rang. "I should have known," I muttered to myself, a little resentfully. But what I heard from the other end made my resentment seem very petty.

"My baby's just died!" the young mother cried at the other end of the line, her usually crisp enunciation blurred by sobs of uncontrollable grief.

I couldn't believe it. Only the previous Sunday I had baptized the child and attended a family party afterwards. I remembered how thrilled the parents were to have received the baby by adoption after waiting so long. That day everything seemed right for them — they had just moved into a handsome new home and, like most young couples, were oblivious to the mortgage they had assumed to buy it. What difference did being in debt make to them? They had everything going for them— or so it seemed. Jacques, the husband, had just been promoted; they were surrounded by family and friends; they felt good about their new church. How could they know that less than a week later their bright, shining world would suddenly go dark?

That was not the only question that consumed me as I drove to their ranch-style bungalow. I wondered what could have happened to take this precious infant's life. She had been so cuddly, so healthy when I had held her at the font just days before. What could I say that would reconcile her baptismal blessing and her sudden fate? I could not think of a word that would do the slightest good. I wanted to turn the car around and go home, go anywhere except where duty called.

When I arrived I found the doctor there too, and was relieved I didn't have to say anything while he made his examination. But he soon left after pronouncing the tragedy a "crib death," a phenomenon medically inexplicable but for which I thought the parents would want a theological explanation.

I could not have been more wrong. Before I could say anything, the father looked at me earnestly and said with a conviction that his French accent enhanced, "It's God's will."

It was no time for debate or even discussion. All I could do was read a passage of scripture, offer a prayer and leave with inner thanks that both parents seemed at peace despite the way life had suddenly tumbled in on them.

But as I drove home I could not get the father's words out of my head. Nor can I now, these many years later, as I think of all the others who have explained mindless tragedies the same way. A friend spat out that conviction at me after I tried to share a word of comfort following his brother's funeral. The manner of his death had defied all reason. While weekending at a small country place he owned, he was struck down from behind by a car as he was cycling along a country road. If it had happened on a busy city street, it might have been understandable. But it made no sense at all on a quiet country road where the only two vehicles were the bicycle and the car. Yet when I told my friend how much I would miss his brother, he shot back, "God never makes mistakes!"

I couldn't believe my ears. Was this man claiming God willed his brother to die this irrational, inexplicable death? How could he think that way? What could make him so absolutely, unconditionally sure that God had arranged this tragedy, as if he were the devil disguised as God?

As I recall those two people, the one a father, the other a brother, I have to ask what kind of God they believed in. What could be right about willing the death of an innocent baby in her crib or a good man on his bicycle? That would put God on the same level as those Nazi officials who, standing at death camp admission gates, decided some people would go straight to the gas chambers, but other arrivals would survive a little longer. Surely many people turn away from believing in God at all because they assume that is the only way of conceiving him. They flatly refuse to trust in someone who, presiding over the world at a cosmic console, pulling out a stop here, pressing down on a pedal there, determines each hapless person's part in this discordant cacophony the human race must endure.

How many of us want to worship that kind of God? Or sing doxologies of praise to one who wills that a car go down a country road precisely at the same time a man is pedalling his bicycle down it too? And with a whole road for the two of them to share, wills that they collide? Instead of worshipping him, I'd rather say, "Keep me out of his way! What kind of killer is this God who we thought was the giver of life? If he were human, he'd be called psychotic and locked up!"

*But Believing
In Nothing is
Not Much Better*

Another friend of mine, who suffers from a neurological disease, illustrates how we are not better off when we simply junk this concept of God and believe in nothing.

She is slowly losing what the doctor calls her motor faculties. She is still able to walk but not easily. She wobbles a bit with every step, almost as though she has to decide whether to make it or not. Her right hand has a tremor bad enough for her to use two hands when she lifts a cup to her lips.

For a formerly vivacious, dynamic young woman, it has been traumatic. She has lost some of her psychological equilibrium as well as some of her physical competence. She now sees herself as no longer the person she was. For a woman who once hosted the most elaborate dinners you could ever wish to enjoy, even pouring a cup of tea is becoming a challenge she has to treat with care.

But the problem is deeper still. The product of an evangelical upbringing, she had sincerely held what she calls a "textbook faith" in God as sovereign over us all. That faith is gone. She sees life now as "just a crap game in which a few lucky ones are winners and the rest of us lose out." For her existence has become mere chance from conception to death.

But thinking that way about herself has not brought her the peace I have found in the people who thought their sorrows were God's will. Just the opposite. She is suffering twice-over, in body and soul. She has lost all confidence that there is someone in charge of the world, and with that all faith that human existence has any meaning.

Her predicament has been called nihilism, a philosophy whose name is taken from the Latin *nihil*, meaning nothing. It is one of the most common philosophies of life held by twentieth century people, and at its core is this conviction that there is nothing that holds everything together.

Today's nihilist is a person who believes that at the center of life there is a great, big nothing. Each of us is just a bit of cosmic dust, blown by chance into the warm sunshine or towards the storm's center. We should not look for meaning in either adversity or prosperity. Instead we should just endure or enjoy it as the case may be. Life is just a crap game.

What a choice we have! Believe in God if we can conceive of him as the divine dictator who moves men and women around like robots, or stop searching for meaning because "there ain't any." Give up wondering why this or that tragedy occurs because there is no explanation. Stop asking questions that simply existence has a meaning somewhere.

What a choice! Believe you are a robot or believe you are a lottery ticket!

Religious people often choose the first because they assume their belief in God as sovereign demands it. They praise the Lord when something good happens and close their minds to what the evils of this world say about this God.

A man wrote to me thus after his wife's death to tell me how good God had been to her right up to the end. Even the end itself, he wrote, was evidence of God's never failing love. What was there about her death that demonstrated God's unfailing compassion to his wife? She had died at the wheel of her car, he wrote, before she backed it out of the driveway onto the street! So she had died quietly instead of being torn apart in a violent accident on the expressway.

That's how he understood life and death at the hands of God, and obviously it gave him peace of mind even in bereavement. But what does it say about God to the rest of us? Is he a God who decides some will die peacefully and others will suffer bloody deaths? Are we like marionettes who move as our divine master pulls the strings? If the answer is "Yes," then we have to face up to what Robert Frost said about him in "The Fear Of God":

31

...an arbitrary god
whose mercy to you rather than to others,
Won't bear too critical an examination.

The best way we can believe in this kind of God is
not to think about what we are believing. Just
believe it, or better still, feel it.

But thinking of this world as a giant lottery can
be just as unsettling. To be fully human we need
meaning in our lives. Many would rather have the
wrong answer than no explanation at all. They cannot bear to think no one is in charge and the world
is like an old-style Wild West town or a modern
inner-city ghetto. They know there is evil in God's
world but they prefer believing it is where he
wants it to be, in defined disadvantaged locations
or among depraved groups.

That belief may give what some of us see as the
wrong meaning of life, but at least it is a meaning
and they cling to it. As they see it, the option of
nihilism means turning this world into a jungle.
They fear our society would become like ancient
Israel when it had no king and people did what
was right in their own eyes (Judges 21:25).

Since nihilism is such a widely held philosophy
of life in the West today, we should take this fear
seriously. If western culture has any dominant
characteristic today, it is the nothingness so many
find when asking what life is all about. Ordinary
people come from nothing insofar as few know
who their ancestors were; a surprising number do

not know who even their grandparents were! The constant mobility of life today means that few sink deep roots. Casual acquaintances take the place of strong family ties and personal relationships. When people face death it is another big Zero, another nothingness to enter like the one being left. To make the dismal picture complete, most of us are forgotten soon after we have left this world. In this day of cremations not even tombstones tell the future that once there were people who bore our names.

That is one reason why many turn to religions that give some sense of identity in the face of nothingness. We all have a basic need to belong to someone and belief in a personal God meets a large part of that need. If this belief demands accepting claims that cannot be held logically, many people wrap their minds around them anyway. For them it is just like eating a fish dinner. The bones can be put on one side of the plate while the fish is enjoyed.

Authoritarian religion, based on its concept of an authoritarian God, has thus not suffered the death of a thousand doubts that many predicted. If it comes to a choice between believing in something and believing in nothing, the something usually wins. But fortunately that is not the only choice we have. It really is not necessary for us to hang our minds up with our hats when we go into a place of worship.

*The Big
Picture*

How do we make any sense out of speaking about God's will when a baby dies in the crib, a decent man is struck down while innocently cycling, a vigorous woman starts to walk as though she were stumbling? The key is connecting a person's suffering to a greater reality — or finding our place in the big picture. As long as an event is isolated it will be misunderstood. But if it can be connected to something greater, we can escape what the German philosopher Georg Hegel called "the abyss of nothingness," and we can do it without turning God into a devil.

We do not have to wear ourselves out struggling over the conundrum of how God could inflict such suffering on ordinary people. What we need is to grasp the context into which our suffering can be fitted, to look at the whole picture of which our life experiences are single pieces. That will not take the suffering away, probably not even reduce its pain. But it will give you and me a way of understanding that will help us cope with our problems.

To find this connection, let's go to the place where I first found it. If any reader is offended because I am starting with philosophy instead of theology, I ask you to suspend judgment for just a little while. Adopt the attitude of St. Justin, the first Christian philosopher and one of the first martyrs.

His attitude was that we should take truth where we can find it. He found truth in the Old Testament so he took it. But he also found it in Greek philosophy and he took that too. Both sources, he claimed, prepared people for the same good news. Truth is truth is truth. So let's see what truth we can find among the Stoics.

These philosophers espoused a message that attracted Greeks and Romans for about 500 years, and still influences you and me today. Stoicism has had such a pervasive influence that its effects have even entered our language. When people do not go to pieces in a crisis, we refer to them as "stoical," this ancient philosophy still standing for an effective way of coping with the troubles of life. So our short drop-in visit on the Stoics will be much more than a tour through a museum of ancient ideas. It will reveal beliefs incredibly up-to-date.

"Trust Nature"

The word Stoic comes from an Athenian building where, about three hundred years before Christ, men gathered to exchange ideas with their teacher, a philosopher named Zeno. Called the Stoa, this beautiful colonnade (now restored near the foot of the Acropolis) was anything but a lecture hall. It was used more for trade than education and was surely the most aesthetically superb marketplace the world has ever seen. Zeno and his friends met

there, and from their dialogues emerged a philosophy that dominated Greek and Roman thinking for
five centuries.

A major reason for its influence was the way it
taught people to face the insecurities of times that
were much like our own. They were times of
expanding, sprawling cities on the one hand and of
collapsing, disappearing communities on the other,
of increasingly rapid communication across an
entire empire and constant strife within local
regions. With their big cities filling up with homeless beggars, with the world where they had been
brought up apparently coming apart, the upper
class elite grasped at a philosophy that gave them a
place to stand. They suffered as much as anyone
else, but the Stoics could not be overcome by their
suffering. Their world could collapse, but they
would remain standing among the ruins.

How did they gain this inner strength?
Fundamental to their philosophy was the maxim,
"Trust nature." By that the Stoics meant that we
should fit ourselves in harmony with the natural
order.

Negative should be integrated as well as positive,
death as well as birth, defeat as well as success, each
pain being seen as much a part of the natural process as good fortune. By doing what comes naturally the Stoics did not mean a person should give full
rein to passions, desires and ambitions.

Excessive lust, greed and envy were contrary to
nature. So was any exaggerated emotion. Stoics

refrained from displaying euphoria when life went their way or shedding copious tears when it turned against them.

What they valued was emotional detachment. They could suffer as much as anyone else, but they did not fear it as much because they had cultivated detachment. The Stoic, said the Roman philosopher Seneca, was not beyond suffering but was above it. No matter what the occasion, the Stoics held some of themselves back. They did not give themselves unconditionally to any relationship or possession. They knew that everything in this life belonged to the natural order and therefore should not be valued too highly. From this detachment they drew the reward of tranquillity, an inner peace in the face of whatever life brought. This they gained by connecting every experience to the total reality, by fitting every piece into the big picture.

Shall we all try to become Stoics? Even if we wanted to, most of us couldn't. We have been encouraged to place unlimited value on making gains — money, status, power, fitness — and to dread their loss as personal failure. We have been encouraged to let it all hang out emotionally, and feeling detached from family and friends is not an idea for most of us.

But the Stoics still have something to teach us about the nature of things. When we learn to trust nature we learn how to connect our lives to an order we cannot escape. We learn that even if all of us could take turns at being God for a day, we would not govern the world differently from the way he has ordained. This must be a world where a baby dies when its breath is cut off no matter how innocent and cuddly the baby is. It must be a world where a man's life ends when his bicycle is struck by a car and his neck is broken. It must be a world where a woman will not walk very well when her nervous system is taken over. These troubles do not result from God looking down on a crib and deciding that baby will die, or that man will hurtle through the air to his death, or that young woman's happiness be truncated.They happen because they are part of a natural world, that would be a far worse world if its order were broken as often as its miracle-seekers want it to be.

Yes, God could have intervened to save each of those three persons. The fact that he did not is enough to turn many people — some believers, some sceptics — away from him altogether. If some of us could be God for a day, we are sure we would intervene for the whole twenty-four hours. We are like a grandmother I know who has renounced her faith because her grandson reacted negatively to an innoculation. The explanation that it happens perhaps once in a thousand times is no comfort. All she can see is the young child harmed because of this medical fluke. "Why didn't God do something?" she laments. "If it had to happen to somebody, why not to me? My life is over. But why a baby? I'll never believe there's a God. No. Not no more!" How many others have you heard say the same thing? Maybe you've said it yourself. It does not matter whether a person is a sophisticated thinker or an unpretentious worker, the message is the same: God should move in when this world goes wrong.

But let's ask ourselves if that is really what we want. What a hopeless world this would be if God intervened as often as people call on him to do! Harsh as the rule of law seems, it is better than its opposite. If this world were not a place where effect followed cause nearly all the time, the world would be a jungle of the unpredictable. Although we do not know what causes crib-death, we do know breathing must go on if life is to continue. We know a man cannot be thrown through the air and land on his head without death or critical injury. We know a person cannot walk easily if her nervous system is not working. But let us suppose we did not know that, or at least could not be sure. Let us suppose there was no cause-effect relationship at work in the human body at all. Let us ask ourselves then how medical science would be possible. Like any other science, it is based on its being able to assume a natural harmony. It depends on doctors being able to assume that what has happened in the past will probably happen in the future. On that basis medicines can be prescribed, surgery can be performed, and treatments recommended. None of that could happen if there were no natural order, no way of identifying patterns in the way the human body acts and reacts.

This assumption of a natural order has to be made in every part of life. Would a farmer plant seed in the Spring, or a commuter turn the key in his ignition, or a surgeon begin an operation, or a researcher record the findings of each experiment, or a mechanic go to work on your car, unless each of them could reasonably expect that what had happened before would happen again? Turn this world into a paradise of miracles and it could become a nightmare.

That is one reason why if you or I could be God for a day, we probably would act about the same as he does every day. We all think we would change everything, but if we became as wise as God we would know the world has to run the way it does if it is to run at all.

I have to admit that sounds most convincing to people not in trouble themselves. When tragedy strikes, especially when it comes without warning, most of us react like the woman who lamented after her teen-age son's death: "Why doesn't God bring him back to life? He raised his own son. Why doesn't he raise mine?" It was a sincere plea from a sincere person who had taught the kindergarten children in my church school with love and tenderness for years. I wanted to take her in my arms and sob with her because I shared her sorrow too. I had known her son, Tom, so well and liked him so much. He was around the church several times a week and was obvious potential for the ministry. I had prepared him for Confirmation and he had served with me at the altar. Like his mother, I too wanted a miracle.

But we both had to accept that Tom, like his mother and me and everyone else, belonged to a natural order and had to leave it as naturally as he had entered it. The Bible's witness to the resurrection of Jesus tells of a unique event for a unique purpose. Jesus was not resuscitated so that he could resume a normal human existence, grow old along with his friends, and eventually die again. Miracles, marvels, prayers, anointings notwithstanding, each human being must accept what nature imposes on us all. We all begin when a sperm fertilizes an ovum and we all end when breathing stops, and blood is no longer pumped through our bodies, and the brain, incredible computer that it is, at last goes "down." Nature has the first and the last word with us all.

But there is one thing we can do about nature. We can control our attitude toward it. The Stoics pointed out that it is we alone who decide how we will react to natural events. We can grieve or we can accept. We can rebel or we can submit. One option will lead to despair. The other, the Stoics claimed, can lead to tranquility. You and I are locked into the natural order but we can choose how we respond to sickness as well as health, death as well as birth, clouds as well as sunshine. We cannot escape them but we can cope with them.

It is counterproductive to rail against the tragedies of existence as though nature ought to reverse itself with you and me or the people we pray for. Tranquility comes from recognizing how nature is neutral as well as orderly. It has no morality and makes no judgments. It cannot pick and choose among people according to our virtues and faults. Its rain, as Jesus reminded people, must fall on the just and the unjust alike. Nature cannot consider the innocence of a baby in the crib or a man on a bicycle or a woman trying to walk straight. As Martin Luther, father of the sixteenth century Protestant Reformation, put it: "Breath is given to the murderer even as he raises his dagger in the air to plunge it into his victim." The natural process works among the evil as much as among the good.

Does that make God, as nature's creator, someone we can't trust? If we answer "Yes," we should also ask ourselves what kind of God we are looking for and what kind of world we think we should have. If it is a world with no rule of law, it is a world all but impossible to conceive. I know that some of us feel, think and pray as though we want that kind of God, but we have not stopped to think what kind of a mad, mad world this planet would become if God acted that way. If nature became our moral judge, the world would become a crazy patchwork quilt where the rain fell only on farms where the farmer was upright. What would the criteria be for earning the rain — or the degree of depravity for losing it? Can we imagine what it would be like to live in a family if sickness came only to those members who were corrupt enough to be punished by God — if health became the prize for star performers in a morality contest? Nature has to be morally neutral. The floodwaters must wash over the innocent just as the nurturing rain must fall on the fields of the unjust.

So the Stoics taught. But so did the Bible too. Jesus drew on nature to illustrate what it meant to live under God's will. Perhaps he learned this message firsthand as a youth walking through the fields near Nazareth under the clear, bright, sharply hued sky over the Galilee where he grew up.

When he became a preacher he urged people to pattern their lives on nature and the way God had created it:

Look at the lilies of the field.
They don't spin cloth. But they are dressed
in clothes more beautiful
than Solomon, in all his regal glory, ever wore!
(Matthew 7:28-29)

He found the same message in the Old Testament, the scriptures in which he had been steeped since he was a boy in the synagogue. From it he learned the wisdom of his people's ancient understanding of how to be truly human by living under God's will. That meant accepting the natural order with its cyclical patterns. As the writer of the book called Ecclesiastes wrote, there is:

a time to be born and a time to die:

a time to plant, and a time to pluck up,
a time to kill and a time to heal,
a time to break down and a time to build up,
a time to weep and a time to laugh,
a time to mourn and a time to dance.
(Ecclesiastes 3:2-4, NKJ)

Tranquility comes from accepting that existence has its negatives as well as its positives. Sorrows are part of this life as well as joys, and when they come, we are foolish people when we curse either God or nature. We are happier people when we accept the clouds as well as the sunshine, and happier still when we recognize the clouds are just as necessary to the "big picture" as the sunshine is.

Without the shade of the clouds or the rain they carry, this earth would become as lifeless as if it had no sunshine. We might wish that God would remove all pain and wipe away every tear. But if God were as foolish as we are, we would learn why the ancient Greeks said that when the gods wanted vengeance against people, they gave them what they had prayed for. If one of us could be God for a day, it would be better for everyone else to keep doing what God has been doing: "Trust nature!"

Trust Providence

Trusting nature was not the whole of Stoicism. The Stoics developed a second message that was even more important to our understanding how the down side of life can be connected to the upside. This was their teaching on providence.

Before we discuss what they meant, however, let's dispose of some misconceptions that have developed in the centuries since the Stoics' time. Many people think believing in providence means believing everything will turn out all right for us in the end. Religious people can make this mistake too. In the Book of Common Prayer, for example, a prayer refers to God's "never-failing providence," clearly implying that when we are right with God, we have an alliance that cannot be stopped. Around the beginning of this century, Christians were so convinced of this that Winston Churchill could begin his history of World War I by referring to the British assumption that providence would always protect their island from disaster. On the other side of the North Sea, however, German Christians believed providence could be counted on to look after Germany when it fought with Britain. The theologian Paul Tillich, himself a German World War I veteran, wrote of how his fellow soldiers assumed piously in 1914 that providence would support their army against harm and defeat.

That was not what the Stoics meant by providence. The word comes from two Latin terms, *pro* and *video*, literally meaning to look ahead. But for the Stoics it meant more than foreknowledge. Centuries before the Stoics, the Greeks had believed this world was not a freewheeling kind of place where people could be masters of their fate and captains of their souls. They believed men and women were subject not only to the gods but to a higher power still. It was fate or destiny, sometimes called by the personal name, Moira. Everyone was ultimately subject to it, as Aeschylus wrote in his play, *The Libation Bearers*, "Destiny awaits the free man as much as the slave."

What the Stoics did was to take this idea up and build on it. They taught that providence — or God, as they sometimes called it — ordained everything that happened to people, good and evil alike. This did not contradict their teaching on nature because like the good, the evil added to the "big picture." Providence meant that everything in existence could be brought together. Every event in your life — so the Stoics claimed — could be seen as a missing piece in this picture.

Stoic tranquility in the face of trouble — the quality that made them so much admired in the ancient world — was based on this belief. The Stoics refused to judge an event on its own but insisted it be fitted into the whole of life. No matter what came or did not come to them, the Stoics were not overwhelmed. They could lose everything else but they could not lose their tranquility as long as they held that belief. This tranquility was not an emotion that could go up and down with their moods. It was a mental attitude founded on a belief.

That belief was all the more impregnable because

it did not depend on evidence. The Stoics did not need to find out how all their experiences were fitting together to make up a harmony. They just believed it and lived in the confidence their belief was true. The result was a kind of courage that fitted Ernest Hemingway's memorable definition, "grace under pressure."

If you or I say some tragedy is God's will, we can mean what the Stoics meant when they spoke about providence. We can mean that somehow, perhaps in a way we will never know, this event will fit together with others to make a harmony. We do not have to mean God put his hand over the mouth and nostrils of that baby to snuff out a tender life. Nor will we mean that God turned a motorist toward a lone bicycle so that my friend would meet such a tragic end. We will certainly not mean that God looked down from heaven and picked a woman out from millions of others as the one he would afflict.

What we can mean is that everything — even these calamities — can be fitted together to serve some good purpose. We do not have to portray God as a monster, ready, willing and able to do things from which any decent man or woman would shrink. We can appreciate how this world has to be a place where those tragedies will be constant travelling companions of the human race. And we will also see how they can be fitted with the good things of life.

History is filled with people who have found

that kind of courage, people who have found problems can be fitted with opportunities. When Victor
Hugo had to leave France because of his attacks on
the Third Empire, he had to spend nearly twenty
years on an island. During that exile, however, he
wrote some of his major works and instead of
looking back on those years with bitterness, commented: "I wrote so much I should have been
exiled years before." Helen Keller pointed out that
her lifelong blindness and deafness not only meant
becoming an inspiration to millions of other disadvantaged people, but gaining an insight into her
own soul that she might not have had if she could
have seen and heard. On the Trans-Canada
Highway north of Lake Superior stands a lonely
statue to mark the point where cancer compelled
Terry Fox to stop his coast-to-coast run on one leg
to raise funds for cancer research and to inspire a
nation to look beyond self-interest. Who would
have ever heard of him if he had been just another
two-legged young athlete? Who would have heard
of Mother Theresa if she had spent her ministry in
a fashionable girls' school instead of in a Calcutta
slum?

The Bible is filled with such stories too. All its
pages have something in common. It is the conviction that regardless of whether people are up or
down, God will fit everything together to serve his
purpose. When the tribes of Judah are to be taken
into exile in Babylon, for example, Jeremiah brings
them a good news message from God that even

this horrendous fate will be used. He tells them:

> I have plans for you...
> I'm going to give you a future
> and I'm going to give you hope.
> (Jeremiah 29:11)

St. Paul saw every experience this way, from the time he was converted to the gospel of Jesus Christ until he wrote his last words. Every event in his eyes was a part of the vocation God had given him. Whether good or bad, it was all part of the grand design God had for the world's salvation. No matter what happened — the physical affliction he called his "thorn in the flesh," or being arrested and kept in chains — St. Paul remained convinced his life was all providential. In ways he might never know, it would fit together. In spite of being in jail when he wrote the Epistle to the Philippians, he could tell his readers:

> I have learned in whatever state I am in to be content.
> I know how to be abased and I know how to abound.
> In any and all circumstances I have learned the secret...
> (Philippians 4:12, RSV)

That secret was what I have called connecting — refusing to understand an event on its own, but instead connecting it to a greater reality.

"Just a moment!" you may be saying to yourself and to me. Is that not ignoring the horrors of this century, horrors of unprecedented scale? Are we expected to believe the Bible wants us to view the Holocaust of the Jews or the killing fields of Cambodia as "connectable" to God's purpose for humanity? What great harmony of human history needed the blood of the sixteen million people that have been killed by arms since World War II? How do we rationalize the deaths of innocent airline passengers blown apart by a terrorist's bomb? There has been so much macro-evil in this century that the rest of this book could be filled if all I did was list horrors inflicted on the innocent. How can they be thought providential?

*The Cross
of Jesus*

To answer that question, I want to share another message. It fits everyone, religious or not, Christian or something else. It fits us all because it is about a person with whom we share our common humanity. We have so identified Jesus with one religion we forget the New Testament presents his message as good news for any one whose life is filled with bad news. I write of Jesus because every act of evil and innocent suffering has been anticipated in his cross. One reason that cross preaches good news is that it offers a message of how meaning can be conferred on the most irrational of acts, and dignity given to the most debased of victims. When we see how the terrifying, tortuous, dehumanizing death of Jesus can still be called God's will, then we see how the same can be said of any other horror that has made its dark way into the world. It may be a baby killed in a gas chamber or a baby who dies in a crib, but these pathetic deaths can be connected with something greater. That is what the cross of Jesus teaches us.

I do not believe that God willed Jesus to be arrested in the dark of night the way the Gestapo arrested their victims centuries later. Nor do I think he willed Jesus be beaten and tortured by soldiers so bored with their tedious duties they took sadistic pleasure in brutalizing the helpless. I do not think God willed the nails be driven into Jesus' weakened hands after they were tied to the cross he had been forced to carry up Calvary hill. Nor do I think God willed a Roman soldier take his spear and plunge it into Jesus' side.

But I can believe the cross of Jesus can be connected to all that led up to it and all that has since followed from it. On its own that cross would just be one more injustice inflicted on a human being in the name of law and order. But when it is connected to the gospel message, it can be affirmed as part of God's plan for humanity.

We see that when we do not confine the gospel to what happened on one day and in one place. I have followed the cross of Jesus as one of hundreds of pilgrims making their way down the Via Dolorosa in Old Jerusalem on a Friday afternoon. I knew and shared with them what the event of the first Good Friday means. But we really know the good news of the cross when we connect it to all the other "crucifixions" that have taken place since then.

The message of the cross of Jesus can be applied to all innocent sufferers. It may be a Chilean student demonstrator who was "scorched" with a flamethrower by Pinochet's soldiers because she did not move fast enough when ordered to move on. Or a man sent to the Siberian Gulag for smuggling Bibles to his church because it was not one registered and approved by the state. Or an author put under the ban by the South African government for writing against apartheid. They all — and countless others — suffer, suffer, suffer. But they do not just suffer. What they did can be connected with what Jesus did. Their sacrifices and pains can fit with all the others that have been part of the human struggle with evil.

The same message also speaks to ordinary people who carry their own kind of cross. Like the families that lose children in infancy or brothers in maturity. Like the people who are struck down without warning or lose their strength just when they need it most.

Although most of my first congregation were young couples who had just bought their first homes in which they would raise their children, it did have some middle-aged people. Among them were a man and woman with a grown-up son in the air force. When he came to church with them while on leave, they glowed with pride. He was the apple of their eyes, the focal point of their lives. They were good people but like most of us were not equipped to cope with the trauma that struck them one night like a hurricane hitting an unsheltered coast. Their son's airplane crashed into the Pacific Ocean off the coast of British Columbia and all the crew were lost.

When I was called to their home that night, they were in shock. They seemed broken people who could not be put together again. Ever. But just the opposite happened. During the year that followed their self-understanding deepened as they came to stand under this personal tragedy. They found a new meaning in their own lives as they reflected on the loss of their son's. They found that meaning when they connected their sorrow to the cross of Jesus. He too was a young man whose life was stolen away in the full flush of his young manhood. As this couple identified their sorrow with his they learned how to live with their own. They then understood the meaning of words they had been saying and singing for so long without seeing how they fitted in with their own existence, such as:

There is a green hill far away,
Outside a city wall,
Where the dear Lord was crucified,
Who died to save us all.

That green hill was no longer far away, no longer a place in Jerusalem at all. It was in their own lives, and they had found salvation by connecting their sacrifice with his.

That couple was not foolish enough to think God took their son from them. Certainly not foolish enough to think God was punishing him or them. Nor did they entertain notions of God deciding to tip their son's aircraft into the sea so that eight young airmen could be drowned as a way of serving some higher purpose. But what they did come to believe was that everything — the cross that had pierced their hearts just like the cross on which Jesus died — could be made to work for their betterment.

I do not know if that is what that baby's father meant that Saturday morning when he told me her death was God's will. But that is what I mean and what you can mean when life crashes in on you.

*Living
By Faith*

How can we gain this trust in providence? The way is simple but not easy. It involves liberating yourself from everything that makes you vulnerable to the slings and arrows that come everybody's way — some sooner, some later.

First we have to liberate ourselves from putting too high a value on the things of this world. The less passionately we yearn for them, the less we are wounded when we lose them or even fail to win them. That does not mean we should not work for them or enjoy them. It just means we realize from the beginning that they can be lost.

Am I writing about money and what money buys? Yes. But I am talking also about "goods" that are not condemned from pulpits, are perhaps even praised there. Knowledge is one that has a high priority on the campus where I have spent most of my adult life. Status is a prize sought by the arts and letters crowd as much as it is by Yuppies of my city. Power consumes the men and women who inhabit the political world where I spent so many years. Fitness has become a craze that has spawned an entire new industry in less than a generation. The hunger of lonely people for relationships is behind almost every new film and television commercial.

Knowledge, praise and status among one's peers, good health — they're all good. But not good enough for the kind of commitment some of us give them. The first step to peace in the midst of suffering is a sense of proportion that frees you from being taken over by some desire. You may still suffer failure but it will not overcome you as a person. Though your whole world crumbles around you, to paraphrase one of the Stoics, you will take it all still standing up.

You should also liberate yourself from thinking there is a believable God only if the innocent never suffer, the wicked always get it in the end, and the good people come out winners. Where did we get this notion that God ever promised us a rose garden? Not in the Bible, nor in the scriptures of any other religion that has commanded faith over the centuries. Their message, in different ways, provides the same truth: evil and innocent suffering are part of life. What faith can do most for us is give us help with coping.

There is an old saying about avoiding doctors who lose most of their patients. Sounds practical, doesn't it, and the same reasoning suggests we should avoid believing in a God who does not protect us in "danger's troubled night." But the reality is that all doctors lose all their patients. All of them die sooner or later. Doctors can only push the fatal day back. They cannot push it off the calendar, not even for themselves. We keep going to them because they help us to cope. So believers in God keep turning to him in prayer and in praise. They realize that they too will suffer just as much as the unbelievers, but their faith brings them something they are better for having.

A television preacher can build up an audience and a revenue by promising more than he — or God — can deliver. Not surprisingly people can give up on the kind of God that preacher proclaims. But not on the kind of God revealed in Jesus on the cross and confessed every time the Apostles' Creed is said, "...was crucified, died, and was buried..." No rose garden there. No easy promises of health, success, happiness, or afflu-ence. The cross of Jesus does not offer one thing western culture prizes. But it does offer what we need when those prizes have nothing left to give us. It is trust that everything can be fitted together.

Maybe you are not ready for that kind of faith. That is a personal decision. But you can still be ready to view everything in your life as "con-nectable" to a higher purpose. You may not know what it is but it is still possible for you to believe it is there. Common sense tells me I am not the center of the universe but just one small part of it. What happens to me should not be judged just on its own, but be connected and fitted into humanity's "big picture." Anyone of us can believe that, and when we do, we have gained the first thing we need for coping with humanity's tireless enemy.

CHAPTER THREE

What Kind of World is This When the Innocent Suffer and the Evil are Rewarded?

I have been a candidate for Canada's Parliament three times, twice successfully. The last contest was the disappointing one, not only for me but also the supporters who worked so hard for me. Not all people saw it, however, the way they did. One man wrote me afterwards to tell me my defeat was really divine retribution! During my years in office I had not persuaded the government to grant him a request on which he had his heart set. He was convinced it was all my fault. Although his letter assured me of his own sympathy, it also claimed that once again God had shown he had his way of getting even with the likes of me. As far as he was concerned, my political death was the wages of sin.

I was impressed, not so much by his bitterness as by his assumption that he was more charitable than

God. As we saw when reviewing the Book of Job, this was not a new thought. Since ancient times there have been people ready to believe suffering must mean the sufferer is being punished. Let a marriage break down, a career take a nose dive, a business go bankrupt, a person get sick — or a politician lose an election — and there is always someone to link it to moral failure.

One of my clerical friends explained the health problems of a fellow minister to me like this: "At the start he was pretty good," he said, meaning he was conservative in Biblical interpretation. "Then he went liberal. It just shows God brings a person down when he falls away."

I was staggered. What God was this? What decent man or woman would widow a woman and orphan two children because a man changed his thinking? How could anyone believe that about a God of justice and mercy?

But I felt even more shock a few years later when my friend's own health fell apart. How does he explain that I wondered. He hasn't gone liberal. Just the opposite. Yet there he is, wife dead, bad heart, near a nervous breakdown. Does he think God is punishing him too?

It is not possible to be logical and infer God is judging a person because that man or woman is having a hard time. "God is smiling on us," a young woman told me happily when I congratulated her and her husband on purchasing a new home. I was glad she thought so, but I had to wonder if she thought God did not smile just as much on the homeless. When Jesus was on earth he was homeless. Did that mean God's face was turned away from him?

My post-election critic was just as barren of logic when he leaped to his conclusion. He could have asked himself questions that would have shown how irrational a judgment he was making. He could have asked himself why the Member of Parliament, who had tried to help him, was defeated, but the cabinet minister who had ruled against him was re-elected. Or he could have wondered why a government, which he considered heartless, was returned with an unprecedented majority. Why was I singled out for this form of political capital punishment?

Protesting that we cannot understand why God chooses to punish this person and not another is a cop-out. If a person's troubles are a divine judgment, why is God so choosy about condemning some sinners and letting others go free? What kind of a world is this when the innocent suffer and the guilty are rewarded? It is not fair to pretend we know God is judging someone, and then protest we really cannot understand the ways of God.

But it is worse than being illogical. To think suffering means sin and success means goodness is an obscenity. It makes God into an evil fiend who can approve prisoners of conscience suffering excruciating electrical torture and send starving people on treks of hundreds of miles to find refuge from famine. Do we really want to believe that kind of God explains this kind of world?

Some people do. Like my fundamentalist friend, some stagger under the burden of thinking their own suffering means God has turned against them. A devout working man lamented to me that his wife had cancer and could not be expected to live. He could not understand what God had against him and her. Had they not come to church every Sunday? Perhaps, he suggested to me, they could come twice. For him God was a judge whom he thought he had appeased by all these years of faithful worship. When he thought of increasing the payment, what was he saying about God? What was he saying about the world God presided over?

It is so easy to think that God is just like so many of us, someone who stores up every grievance and lies in wait for the right moment to even the score. Or to think God is someone who can be bought off with gifts, service, cajolery. If he were like that, God would be a judge, but an indictable one. Why then do we insist on beating one another over the head with theologies that suggest he is?

Theology
as Anthropology

One answer was given early in the nineteenth century by Ludwig Feuerbach (1804-72), a German philosophical critic of religion. It is not about God at all, he insisted. It is about humanity. What sounds like theology is really anthropology. Humanity is not made in God's image. God is made in humanity's.

This was not a new idea. One of the early Greek philosophers claimed that if cattle had gods, they would look like cows. Feuerbach's critique of religion was more profound than that, and it helps us to understand why we think God is the kind of sadistic judge some people think he is. So let's reflect a little bit on his theory of religion.

He argued that all people have an image of the perfect being they would like to be, and belief in God offers them a giant screen on which they can project this image. Feuerbach did not mean that you and I think up the idea of God ourselves so that he would be what we wanted him to be. Feuerbach did not mean that each of us imagines we are divine. What he meant was that each generation accepts our society's tradition about God because it meets a genuine human need. Inherent in each of us is a desire to be what we are not. Conceiving God as the perfect being is a way of projecting what we cannot achieve ourselves but want to believe exists. God is thus a human being whose attributes have been extended to the *nth* degree.

This explains why many of us go on believing a theodicy that logic should compel us to reject. We can pour all our frustrated resentment and anger into an image of a vengeful God. In time of war we can conceive the enemy's defeat as God judging the wicked and avenging the righteous. In time of peace we can reason that our affluence is due to God blessing us. We want to think our country has been victorious or that our business has succeeded because "somebody up there likes us."

Or coming closer to the concern of this chapter, we can believe just the opposite — that somebody up there dislikes us. Part of the mystery of humanity is how many people have a masochistic desire to suffer, especially to suffer punishment. Some people even seek out suffering at the hands of others and enjoy it all the more if they can think it is punishment. A man or a woman may hire a member of the opposite sex to administer beatings just for this strange satisfaction. Others may play games of dominance and submission so that this pleasure of suffering is enjoyed, at least in fantasy.

As well there are people with a hypersensitivity to guilt. Every human has a capability to feel guilty but some feel it more than others. For them religion means worshipping a God who meets their peculiar need for a wrathful judge. What this can mean to people is that when they see others suffer or endure pain themselves, the explanation of guilt is the first one that they grab. Some citizens are not satisfied with a government that is not harsh and severe with offenders.They are just as unsatisfied with a religion that does not preach God as being a moralistic dragon breathing out fire on everyone.

Alex had spent years faithfully looking after his

chronically ill wife. In spite of his devotion to her there had been times, however, when he could not take it any longer. He grew tired of living in what seemed like a nursing home. He wanted to live like other men his age. Yet he could not deny he had a duty to his wife. This inner conflict drove him sometimes to wish his wife were dead. Then he could be free at last.

But when she did die, he did not find freedom at all. Just the opposite. He could not forget the times when he had wanted her dead. He felt as though he were responsible for her death. Instead of feeling free, he found himself bound to his guilt as tightly as he had been bound to his wife.

This guilt was impossible for him to live with. He wanted to be punished so that he could get it off his back. Alex believed he deserved to be punished. How could his wife lie under the cold ground while he walked about in the sunshine. Before long he became ill. No medical care could relieve him of the illness that now plagued his life. He went to many doctors but none could help him. The reason was that Alex was unconsciously punishing his soul by afflicting his body. Only when later he learned to believe in a God who accepted him, guilt and all, was Alex able to accept himself, guilt and all. Then he recovered his health.

What if he had not learned that good news? He might have taken to his bed for the rest of his days. Or if forced to work, gone through life down on himself, convinced he was unworthy, unable to make himself worthy in God's eyes or his own. What would Alex have been like then?

He would be like people you may know. Perhaps like you yourself. It is so easy for some of us to imagine that God is as hard to please as we are, so easy to think he comes down on us and everyone else the way we do. If there is sickness or hardship or setback, the answer is always the same: God is punishing sinners.

But realism should tell you and me the world is not like that. It is not a place where only the guilty suffer and the innocent are always rewarded.

My Brother
Shows This

If I needed any proof of that, I would have to look no further than my brother, Benjamin. My earliest memory of Ben is a Christmas morning when he pushed me out of the bed we shared to bring back our Christmas stockings from the tree. Big brothers do that sort of thing. But they do other things as well. He taught me how to ride a bicycle. More important, he pressured my parents into sending me to an academic high school instead of a technical one. It was one of the significant turning points of my life and he had the biggest part in it.

But things did not go that well for him. I can remember as if it were yesterday his coming home from work to tell us that, as he was walking across the street during his lunch break, he suddenly found he could not move one of his feet. He literally had to reach down and lift it up to the sidewalk. After a series of medical tests he was told he had what is now called multiple sclerosis. He was eighteen.

Since then his life has been scourged by this invincible enemy. Throughout his early adult years the disease plateaued for long periods so that he was able to marry, raise a family, and hold a job. But he could not enjoy a normal life in a normal way. The sclerosis slowly but inexorably fastened its grip on his nervous system more and more. His walking became so uncertain he had to use a cane, then a brace, and at last a wheelchair. To get himself to work he had to outfit his car with manual controls. It was traumatic to drive through a big city's rush hour twice a day like that, but he did until he could go no longer. Then followed a few years at home until at last hospital care was the only option. He has been in hospital ever since.

There were pluses during the years of struggle. His wife was a model of devotion in sickness and health, prosperity and adversity. He could take pride in four children graduating from university. The family home was paid for. By the time he had to leave work, he had earned a pension large enough to support himself.

But during all those years of achievement, Ben's physical struggle continued like a war that would not end. His body was like a country that was penetrated by an invader whose advance might be slow, but was inexorable. It would have been a blessing if he could have kept enough freedom at least to walk around. But he now lies in bed barely able to turn his head.

Shall we say God is punishing him? If we do, why him? Why not me? Why not you? And for what? What could Ben have possibly done to merit this kind of sentence?

There are no answers to those questions. They are worth asking, though, because they drive us to see that this world does not have a simple justice system that guarantees only the guilty suffer and the innocent always go free. Often, so very often, we cannot make any sense out of what happens to people. Or trace any pattern. Or line up causes and effects. This is a world where you and I cannot always understand evil and innocent suffering. Nor can we always overcome them. So much of the time all we can do is cope with them.

What else can we conclude when we think of all the innocent people who suffer in ways that could not be demanded by any wrong they may have done? Can we think otherwise when we picture a prisoner of conscience in a political prison, vainly trying through the night to draw some warmth from a threadbare blanket or in the morning to gain sustenance from a dry crust and thin tea as he begins another day of hard labor? Is God one of his judges as he walks to his death some morning, just another nameless victim who will be unremembered except in his loved ones' hearts and in the state police computer?

That is not what the Bible tells us about God. Just as Job refused to accept his friends' prattling about divine judgment, so none of us need to take this excuse for a theodicy seriously.

My brother is not in his hospital bed because of judgment. This world is not that kind of a place. It's a world where sinners keep fit, achieve success, enjoy affluence and die surrounded by their families. So do innocent people, but not more than the others. This is a world where there is no necessary connection between the kind of person you are and the kind of life you have.

But there is life-changing value in recognizing that. It could be the opening sentence in a sufferers' manifesto: "Sufferers of the world unite! You have nothing to lose but your guilt." That's not meant to be flippant, still less cynical. It's meant to convince you that, if you are in trouble now, chances are you should not feel guilty about it.

You see others jogging or swimming lengths and you can barely get around. You look at others climbing the ladder, moving to prestigious address-es, taking trips to exotic places. All you can do is struggle to pay your bills. They have such happy homes, but you cannot prevent your marriage breaking down. No wonder you feel guilty.

But you shouldn't. This is an uneven world. One brother gets multiple sclerosis and the other is given health. One soldier is killed before he hits the beach and the man beside him goes through the war without a scratch. Jesus is crucified and Stalin dies in bed. The last assumption we should have when life goes against us is that we have done something to deserve it. Most of the time we haven't.

But there are times when human suffering is the result of men and women not living the way rational human beings should. Some of it should make us feel guilty. More important, it should drive us to relieve it and prevent it. This is a world where some of our suffering is brought on ourselves.

We Hurt
Each Other

It's a world where we hurt each other as well as ourselves. The suffering innocent people endure could often be prevented if other women and men treated them as human beings.

The tobacco smoker who risks his or her life by inhaling tars and nicotine also puts other people at risk. According to medical research reports, this threat of "second-hand smoke" is as great as the hazard to the smokers themselves.

That is only one example of how a person's death may be the wages of someone else's sin. War screams this message at us, few of the killed or wounded or dislocated having any real say in whether the war would be fought or not. We are part of each other, for worse as well as for better. When excessive alcohol abuse leads to sclerosis of the liver it means not only death for the drinker but potential poverty for the dependents. When lust for industrial development threatens the ozone layer that protects the planet from the sun, potential catastrophe for the unconsulted masses as well as for the informed decision makers.

This is because of a law of life that rules us as surely as the law of gravity. It is the law of consequences, the law that dictates a farmer cannot reap what has not been sown, that effect usually follows cause. As the early years of the computer age summed it up, "garbage in" leads to "garbage out." This law applies to you and me in our private lives and also our social behavior. The law of consequences applies to both individuals and societies.

It even transcends space and time. If inferior construction and inadequate safety standards are permitted in building a nuclear energy plant, a breakdown will affect more than the people who built it and the people who work in it. Winds that ignore national boundaries and need no passports to travel carry radioactive particles that contaminate drinking water on the other side of the world. When one generation deforests its land, the next generation will confirm the Bible's warning that the sins of the fathers will be visited on generations yet to be born.

As we have seen there is innocent suffering — like my brother's — that can be blamed on no one.

But this is also a world where much of our suffering can be avoided if we stop when the law of consequences warns us somebody's going to get hurt. Not all our pain is beyond our control or our understanding. Nor do we have to look only to God to explain all of it. Some of it is all of this world. It is a world where people hurt each other. It always has been. It always will be.

That gloomy realism has often caused people to protest: "Yes, that's the way it is. But why must it be that way? Why did God make this world a place where so many wrong choices could be made? Why did he make it a world where the innocent suffer the consequences of the guilty?"

Maybe you've asked those questions yourself. I certainly have. I have wondered why God did not bias us humans to make only right choices that would lead to good consequences. If he had, there would be no wars or pollution or poverty or any of the other kinds of suffering that result from people making wrong choices. Sounds good, doesn't it? But would you really want God to have created the world that way? Would I, if I stopped to think how the cure would be worse than the disease?

Who would want to be a robot able to act only as God had programmed us? As robots you and I would not be able to sin — but we would not be human either. The freedom to choose — even the wrong choices — is essential to being a human. Have you read about planned societies such as those described in the novels *Nineteen Eighty Four* and *Brave New World*? Their people do not seem like people. They have bodies but not souls. They have no freedom to choose and are doomed to live in a world where humanity has been planned out altogether.

That's surely why so many people, in what were once Iron Curtain countries, actually glow when they speak of their newly-found freedoms. As we who have always lived in democracies cannot know, they know what it means to live where someone else calls all the shots. What was proffered as a planned society quickly showed it was a controlled society, where no one but the controllers were living the way men and women should.

That's the kind of world we would have if it had been created the way some think God should have made it. A true humanity demands we are able to choose even when we are wrong. If it were not for that we would be just like the animals with whom we share the world. They live by a form of "programming" inside them — instincts, passions, appetites, habits. Yes, we share all those with them because we are also part of their animal kingdom. But we have something that makes us unique as humans among all the creatures of the earth. It is our freedom to choose.

What a price we pay for it! The price of all the wrongs we do to each other, as well as those we bring on ourselves. But the price of losing that freedom would be higher still. This must remain a world where people can hurt one another.

According to Christian theology, the reason we misuse our freedom and hurt each other is "original sin." That is the belief that each person has a built-in bias to being selfish. This leads us to do the wrong things we do even when we know better. From primeval times people have shown this bias and we have not gotten any better as the centuries have advanced. It is part of our being, not just to choose but to be biased towards making the selfish choice.

That is not a difficult belief to hold when we examine the record of the twentieth century and find there has been no moral progress to keep pace with our technological advance. But it is not the only explanation for this world being like it is.

The doctrine of original sin tells us humanity is what theologians call "fallen," that is, fallen from the high level that God intended in the creation. But according to the doctrine of creation, people are also "finite," and I wish theologians would start stressing our human finiteness as much as our fall from grace. Much of the hurt we cause each other is not just because we are sinners who make selfish choices, but because we are finite people who make mistakes. That is why we have two kinds of evil in the modern world that do tragic harm to innocent people.

*Technological
Evil*

One of them we can call technological evil because

it is a product of this age being dominated by technology. That dominance has brought us great benefits, and without it we might not be able to meet the needs of this world's escalating population. But technology has its down side too, not just because people use it sinfully but because we use it as finite men and women with limited intelligence, knowledge and wisdom. Technology is advancing at incredible speed, but we aren't, and it is therefore a cause of evils so enormous they can scarcely be conceived.

Let's picture a supertanker setting out from port. It is a technological marvel, a floating electronic village. But incredibly it founders in spite of its "traffic lane" being miles wide. Thousands of gallons of oil are spewed into the ocean, bringing death to fish and birds and ruin to people who make their living from the sea. How could it happen when the ship's equipment was so advanced? Something went wrong with the human element, the one on which the most sophisticated technology depends as much as old-fashioned sailing vessels did.

Or let's think of another way technology has become a source of evil. Our need for its benefits is so great, we err in allowing it to expand and expand. Sprawling metropolitan areas become smog-ridden when the number of vehicles outgrows the atmosphere's capability. Once comfortable neighborhoods become uninhabitable when traffic noise rises above what people can bear. Excessive packaging in our throw-away culture has created a garbage disposal crisis in every major center. Beautiful as they are, our cities are dying and technology is killing them. This is not because our leaders and citizens are depraved as much as it is because all of us are finite. We have not measured the harm our choices will cause.

Part of the explanation is that our objectives are good. No one can say it is wrong for coal miners to want work. But acid rain has become a threat to the trees and waters of the Great Lakes region because the wind carries sulfur dioxide exuded by industries that burn soft coal. To cite another example, let us recall how it seemed wonderful just a few years ago when insecticides were developed to rid our farms and homes of pests. They did their work well, both killing the bugs and increasing the crops. But washed by the rain into the streams from the fields where the spraying had been done, these insecticides found their way into drinking water. Obviously they did good, but they also threatened life. At first we finite people felt so good about them. Later we understood.

Should God have deprived us of the potential to develop the kind of technology we have? Nonsense. A moment's thought about the world returned to the age before the Industrial Revolution would show that. But the threat of technological evil in this modern world is enough to make us wary.

We should not challenge God when a spaceship crashes due to a technical malfunction. But we can become more alert to the terrifying capacity for error in us humans, and what that can lead to when we are working with technology.

After an air raid during the London blitz in World War II, someone scrawled on a wall: "What a God!" But someone else drew a line through "God" and wrote "world." That's the challenge of our time: "What a world!" It is a world where technology makes evil possible on a scale no previous age could have imagined. "What a world!"

Institutions Too
Can Be Evil

Along with technology our age,has become dominated by giant institutions — big government, big business, big labor, big shopping, big hospitals, big education, big military, and in some places also big religion. When the world has almost six billion people there is scarcely an alternative. Yes, there is a place for the individualist, but humanity really depends on its institutions.

Their growth has not been all for the good though. They have opened up a new source of evil, and some of the worst problems you and I have can be traced to the way institutions work. Let me tell you a real-life example.

It involves a large corporation, the kind so many people work for. It is a good company that has provided thousands of jobs and satisfied millions of customers. But being an institution means it often acts as if it were not human and were not made up of humans. Marion's story makes that point.

At the time she was in her fifties, a widow whose house was not quite paid for and who had one child still at home. To keep it all going she needed her job. It was like a fire and a flood, therefore, when she heard she was about to be terminated. Yes, she was only one of several hundred being let go. But she was only thirty-five days short of being eligible for a pension. Minimal as it would have been it would have been enough, when added to her other income, to make ends meet. Without it she would lose her home. Marion knew that at her age, she could not get a job paying more than the minimum. Friends told her that surely something could be done. So she decided to have a try.

She went to her manager. He assured her he understood because he was about the same age. But, his comfortable, comforting, roly-poly appearance notwithstanding, he told her he couldn't do anything for her. He explained the whole thing by quoting the company's policy manual to her. One reason he had risen to management was that he had always gone by the book, and he intended to stay in management that way.

He reminded her the union had a grievance procedure, and with that small crumb of encouragement in her, Marion went to her steward. She too was about Marion's age and felt badly about her plight. "I tell you what," she said. "You've never asked the union for anything before. I'll ask our local president if she can do something for you."

It sounded good to Marion, who was so unaccustomed to the ways and wiles of management and labor that she thought anyone called a president must surely be able to help her. But it did not work out that way. All the union leader told the steward was that the company was not contravening the contract. "I know that already," Marion protested when she got the message. But the steward did not offer to be her advocate again.

"Why don't you write the company president?" her daughter suggested. Unassuming and unassertive, Marion was shocked by the idea. She had never seen him. Did not know his name. Did not even think of him. Under normal circumstances she would not have even considered approaching him. But what could she lose now? So the two of them sat down at the kitchen table and the daughter, filled with university campus confidence, wrote a letter and Marion signed it. It sounded so reasonable and impressive — especially its reference to "natural justice" — that she was sure it would persuade this mighty man to help her.

To make sure he got it she decided to deliver it herself. It was a little frightening and also exciting to take the elevator to the executive floor, so quiet, so peaceful in contrast to all those below it. There was such a nice receptionist there, too, that Marion was glad she had come. But she still did not meet the man she wanted. She learned he was away visiting another part of his corporate empire, and she had to make do with giving it to the receptionist, who graciously but firmly barred her from going any further.

Marion hoped her letter really would reach the great man's hands. She could not know the closest it would come was his administrative assistant. After reading it, she just handed it to her secretary to write Marion a reply explaining the policy all over again. The president's signature was written at the bottom of the letter — appropriately, by a machine.

The evil in all this was the way Marion was not treated as a person. Nor did the officers of the company and union act as persons. Everything about the way both institutions operated was designed to pretend no human beings were involved. Significantly they made as little use of names as possible, making references to one another usually by impersonal titles like chief, boss, president. Even more significant was the way each officer referred to the company manual as though it had a quasi-personal identity. They thus spoke like this: "Policy says...Policy won't allow...Policy has not given discretion..." What a world this is when a person can be treated like a thing, and a book can be treated like a person!

This is because these people were not functioning primarily as men and women. They were acting out roles as officials, workers, agents, each one being understood almost exclusively in terms of an institutional role.

What kind of world is this? It is a world where

people lose some of their humanity every day they live, move and have their being within institutions. The worst part of it is there is no exit from them. Even death is taken over by a coalition of institutions who see to it that the man or woman who has been held in their grip from infancy will not gain freedom even in death.

Nature too
is Evil

But all the evil in this world is not due to people. Some of it is in nature too. The harassed urbanite may find peace on a walk through the woods but the same woods can be an arena of fear for every bird and animal alerted against attack from other creatures.

How is it possible for the world itself to spawn evil? Human free will is no explanation. What can rationalize evil in a created world?

The answer should not be calling them "acts of God," the way insurance policies often do. Even a cursory study of nature shows that God does not arbitrarily decide now and again to send a natural disaster our way. Negatives of nature result from natural elements combining in destructive ways.

Let me illustrate with a little discussion about hurricanes. All I knew about them until a few years ago was that they happened somewhere else. But when my wife and I bought a condominium in

Florida, that changed. Usually hurricanes came close enough only for us to feel the brush of their sleeve as they marched darkly up the Gulf. But the sight was awesome enough to send me to a library so that I could read a little about them.

I learned that hurricanes almost always happen in certain parts of the world: in the North Pacific where they are called typhoons, in the Indian Ocean where they are termed cyclones, and around the Caribbean Sea and Gulf of Mexico. They are conceived from an unlikely but natural marriage between warm air and cool water. Their coming together produces enough vapor to produce one of nature's children of wrath. Elliptical in shape, a hurricane is formed by wind and rain swirling around a stable center called the eye. Inside these storm clouds, called walls, the wind blows at speeds of seventy-five miles or more per hour. Nothing can stop this gargantuan force but nature itself. Once the hurricane leaves the water and strikes land, it begins to lose the supply of vapor on which its life depends, and eventually it dies.

What do these scientific facts tell us about natural evil in a created world? They teach us that hurricanes are not acts of God but are the result of natural forces combining in a patterned way. What I have written about hurricanes applies equally to any other phenomenon. So reality demands we face up to living in a world where nature too is a source of evil and can tear up the home of a working family more easily than the luxury hotel of the affluent.

*What Difference
Does Believing Make?*

What kind of world is this? It's a wonderful world. That's why most of us want to stay in it as long as we can. But it's also a world where the innocent suffer and the guilty are rewarded. Sometimes we do not know any reason that can make sense out of a person's pain. Sometimes it's due to the law of consequences, someone's selfishness hurting others as well as himself. At other times it's due to a human error, our finite minds not being capable of keeping technology error-free and fail-safe. And sometimes it's because we are locked into institutions that make us forget we are people. Innocent suffering comes even from nature running amok.

If all that's true, how can we fit it together with a loving God? How can we believe when we live in a world like this? Obviously we can't if we insist on believing only in a God who will prevent suffering unless it is to punish people like Adolf Hitler. But that is not the only God we can believe in.

We can believe in a God who shares our pain with us. That's the message of the cross of Jesus. It's the message of the prophet Isaiah who wrote about a servant who suffered himself so that others could be healed. It's the message of Gautama Buddha, who first found enlightenment when he encountered the suffering of this world. It is only the spiritual scam artists that tell us God guarantees a pain-free life to those who believe in him. Witnesses to truth are also witnesses to reality. Faith will not keep suffering away from the innocent, nor prevent the guilty from being rewarded. But trusting in a God who shares our pain can help us in another way.

It can help us to cope. We cannot escape from suffering, but we can struggle with it. We cannot prevent it from afflicting us, but we can prevent it from overcoming us. During the years my brother has lost more and more of his bodily control. The marvel has been that he has lost none of his identity as a person. He still sees himself as the head of his family, remains up-to-date on what each of his adult children is doing, and is surrounded by pictures of his grandchildren. Unlike some sick people who become totally absorbed by their condition, Ben remains concerned about the world, follows the news every day, and is not slow about telling his brother what he thinks of it all. But most impressive of all is the way he retains his hope in the future.

In spite of every effort to stop the sclerosis failing, he has never lost the belief deep in his heart that some day he too will overcome. Every news item about research has been seized with eagerness that it might open the door so long shut tight against him. A support group of other MS sufferers was joined so that he could draw encouragement from knowing he was not alone in this relentless struggle. A healing fellowship at his church provided teaching, prayer and spiritual reinforcement. But as far as his physical condition was concerned, there has been no change except for the worse. Many friends joined my mother, when she was alive, in faithfully praying for him every day. Obviously none of it has worked, if by that we mean effected a cure. Neither science nor spirituality has been able to turn the sclerosis back nor even stop its advance. But let us realize that would have been the case had none of these efforts been made. Ben would be in the same condition if he had sought the false haven of cynicism and despair, as beaten in soul as he is afflicted in body. Instead he has gained something precious to him and all who care about him.

Through all this struggle his faith in God has yet to waver. Always spiritually oriented as the most "churchy" of the family, at no time has he doubted God's reality or challenged his integrity. Neither has he criticized his church or its clergy for representing a God so obviously unable or unwilling to cure him. He has continued to worship in his hospital bed as devoutly as he ever did in his parish church. "Why?" is an understandable question in view of the apparent lack of an answer to his prayers. But he can give an answer to it. One day he shared it with me: "I think my faith has helped me put up with all this." A simple, unpretentious claim, but coming from the bed that has held him bound so many years, it was a witness more compelling than any proclamation from prestigious pulpit, stadium rally, or television studio — especially when his respiratory system had become so weak I had to press my hand down on his diaphragm to push enough air up to his larynx for him to be heard.

My brother is no fool when he clings to the hope he may even now be cured. He is not living in a dream world. He knows the odds quite as well as any of his family and friends. But he also knows what you and I should know too. We are never lost until we become losers. The present is never hopeless until we give up on the future. By believing, Ben remains a person. If he gave that up he would be just a patient.

There is a message here for people who are having a soul-destroying struggle, people who wonder how they can believe in anything — even themselves. Maybe you're one. Or you have someone close to you who is like that. Take this to heart. Believing is always better than not believing. Even in a world like this.

It may not bring a cure, restore a loved one, win a victory, or avert an evil. But don't give it up. It will give you something that each of us needs when we are about to drown in a sea of troubles. It cannot always change the world you live in. But it can always change you.

Keep
Fighting

But being a believer does more for you than make you someone who can grin and bear it. As Ben puts it, his faith has helped keep him fighting. He may be losing the fight, but he is not giving it up.

In a world like this, it is absolutely imperative we have that kind of faith. Throughout history it has always been the believers, not the doubters, that found the solution, discovered the breakthrough, charted the course. As George Santayana wrote in "O World Thou Choosest Not:"

Columbus found a world, and had no chart
Save one that faith deciphered in the skies.
To trust the soul's invincible surmise
Was all his science and his only art.

To labor in a research laboratory demands a scientist believe a cure is possible. To work patiently at an arms control conference demands a diplomat believe governments will one day see reason. To lift oneself out of poverty demands a young person believe the door of opportunity can be opened. To make fingers move and feet walk and lips talk demands a stroke victim believe the effort can succeed, at least a little.

Believing is more than agreeing with creeds or holding ideas. It means being motivated. It means putting psychological fuel in your personal tank. It can drive you forward. Without it you will come to a dead stop.

When I mentioned the title of this book to a friend, he commented that I should put the word "Not" after "I." He was partly right. If we stop believing, we will condemn the world to being like this forever. Perhaps worse.

But if we believe we can make it even a little better for ourselves and others, we will.

CHAPTER FOUR

Must We Just Suffer or Can it Make Us Better People?

Of all the attempts to justify innocent suffering, the one that gives me a mental headache is the claim we need to suffer in order to build our characters up.

This belief is held by people who are possessed by the idea that pleasure cannot teach you and me anything good. Only pain can. If they hear about children really enjoying themselves at school, they are sure it's evidence the schools are no good. They recall the days when the strap ruled and children spent their days learning what they didn't like. One man said to me that if he controlled the curriculum in our schools, he would find out what the students disliked the most. "Then I'd give them lots of that!"

He was only one of many I've met who are convinced we should want to suffer in order to

improve. Some, like Robert Browning, have rev-
elled in this belief. In "Rabbi ben Ezra" this nineteenth century English poet wrote:

> ...welcome each rebuff
> That turns earth's smoothness rough,
> Each sting that bids nor sit nor stand but go.
> Be our joy three-parts pain.

Although they do not say that pain is punishment,
they insist it is necessary for character building.
Why should anyone, they ask, argue against a good
God allowing it? Even seeing that we get enough to
make us better people?

Why indeed, since the claim is half-true?
Suffering can be a teacher and I have learned more
from setbacks than successes. Job was a righteous
man, but he understood neither himself nor God
until he found himself down and out. There is
something about achievement and affluence that
make us want to say, like the ancient Israelites, our
power and the might of our own hands has gotten
all this (Deuteronomy 8:17). But let the opposite
happen. Let us lose it all and, like Job, we will see
how dependent and vulnerable we always were.
Humility will take the place of arrogance, and we
will judge others less as we learn how it feels to be
judged ourselves.

But it is only a half-truth. Job is the only one in
his book who grows as a person. His wife and
friends remain just what they had been before —

only more so. The same is true in life today, as I learned through repeated visits to a young parishioner who had been incarcerated in his bed for years by rheumatoid arthritis. Jim was a pathetic sight. Not only were his joints swollen, but his body was twisted as if it had been drawn on a rack. It was my duty to take him Holy Communion regularly but I shrank inwardly from having to look at his skeleton of a frame. The skin was barely stretched over the bone; his teeth protruded through his shrunken face; his long fingers stood uselessly upright as if they were sentries on guard but unable to shoot.

Yet I also looked forward to going to his parents' small apartment above a store on a busy thoroughfare, its constant traffic the only background music for the liturgy I offered. Why? Because Jim always cheered me up. I who went as the bearer of good news always received good news. I knew he liked seeing me and appreciated receiving the sacramental body and blood of another young man who had suffered. But he gave as well as received. Each time he shared with me the unspoken courage he had developed in that lonely room, his only companions his mother and father.

I tell you about him partly to tell you also about them. Their reaction to their son's plight was just the opposite to his. They were bitter against both God and humanity because of what had happened to their son and, I had to suspect, because of what had happened to them. I could not judge them. In fact I had to admire them for their steadfast loyalty to his care. But I also had to note how they did their duty with small grace, and added no cheer to his cheerless days.

His story and theirs is what this chapter is about. Jim obviously developed a deeper character than he might have had if he had remained strong and lithe enough to race about the city in a delivery truck like most of his boyhood friends. But just as obviously his mother and father were not up to their challenge as he was to his. When later they stood with me at his grave side, there were no illusions. The years with Jim had been all cross and no crown. In that shambles of a youthful body a beautiful soul had been shaped. But in their years of frustration an invincible bitterness had taken whatever atom of spirit had been theirs at the beginning of the long watch.

Evil and innocent suffering are part of this world, and as in a mystery, they motivate some people to scale the heights of greatness while they beat others down to the ground.

Does God Afflict Us
to Teach Us?

Since some people like Jim do grow through suffering, it is often claimed that God sends it to us as a way of teaching us what we would not learn otherwise. It's a plausible belief and the sacred writings of many religions teach people that suffering can be instructive. Both Jews and Christians, for example, can read about the value of God chastening his people. The history of Israel and Judah in Biblical times shows how that chastening was often seen as defeat, setback and even exile for his people. The story of the apostolic church was also told in terms of God's servants growing in their faith through suffering.

But as Jim's parents demonstrated, suffering can be counterproductive as a way of educating people. Our prisons are filled with inmates who have been behind bars before. In our hospitals, many patients exemplify just the opposite to courage, cheer and confidence. During the years I pastored a congregation I found no correlation between suffering and character. For every person I found bearing a cross with apostolic courage, I found someone else weighed down with its burden. If we are going to insist innocent suffering is God's way of teaching people the way to live, we had better face up to his needing a better way of doing it.

Instead, why don't we just abandon the whole notion that God sends us afflictions? There is no more reason to think he afflicted my brother with multiple sclerosis than to believe God deliberately spared the rest of us. Certainly the value of character development should not impress us as justification for what has happened to him. There is no doubt Ben has deepened his character through all these years of struggle. But which of us in our right minds would think that has been worth what he has been through? If God wants to teach us how to be truly human, surely there must be a better way he could find.

So let's give up picturing God as the ultimate Mr. Murdstone caning David Copperfield's juvenile bottom in Charles Dickens' timeless novel. Let's see that God is not a Victorian parent stalking the world to see whom he can abuse.

Instead let's see that suffering is as much part of existence as air is part of the world. It goes with being human. Its uneven distribution is as natural as the unequal division of intelligence, strength and skill. When our lives take a downer, we should not praise God for teaching us a lesson. Nor should we resent him for a lesson we would rather have done without. Instead let's see that we live in a world where suffering is part of life. Often there is no reason to justify it. Nor even explain it.

A few years ago I slipped on the ice as I walked to my parliamentary office in Canada's capitol, Ottawa. One moment I was stepping along spryly, my mind filled with Monday morning thoughts about all I was going to do that week. The next moment I was laid out on the sidewalk, my left wrist broken and twisted. I write of it now because the whole experience illustrates my point.

It certainly was not that God made me slip on the ice. My point is that this kind of mishap is as much part of a city's day as getting to work is. The hospital where I went was obviously organized for a certain number of slippery sidewalk victims. It had to be. In an urban winter some people are going to fall, while most walk blithely to work accident-free. Evil is as much a part of life as good is, and is just as unevenly distributed.

If your life has taken a downturn, can you see it that way? It's better if you do. Feeling sorry for yourself will give you the sympathy of just one person. Blaming someone else for your trouble will not change your situation. There is something else that will be much better for you. It is turning your suffering into learning. The way to do it is through two laws of life. Follow them and even your downturn can become an upturn.

The Law of
Compensations

The first one is the the law of compensations. Whenever I suffer a loss, I remind myself that I probably can add a gain I would not have had otherwise. So very often one door closing in my face makes me turn to another door I would never have tried.

I first learned about this law from my college principal when I was a student. He told me about Ralph Waldo Emerson's essay, "Compensations," and suggested I let it guide me through life. It was good advice because the Sage of Concord, as Emerson was often called, offered a message that can make all the difference when trouble comes:

Every excess causes a defect; every defect an
excess.
Every sweet has its sour; every evil its good...
For everything you have missed, you have
gained something else;
And for everything you gain, you lose something.

Emerson was right. None of us can have everything, do everything, be everything. We must pay a
price for everything we gain, and it is often the price
of giving up our chance for something else.

That was what Fred learned when he suddenly
lost his job. Being let out is always a shock but it
was more so in his case. Fred had been doing well
and less than two years earlier had been promoted
to executive status. Against his wife's warnings he
had bought a larger house in a prestige neighborhood and felt confident that increased earnings
would carry the debt load. Why not? He was good
at his job and worked hard at it. He was so preoccupied with it that he seemed a charter member of
the "Thank God It's Monday So I Can Go Back To
Work Club." When a corporate takeover led to a
restructuring, Fred learned how none of his efforts
for the former owners meant a thing. He was out.

What shocked him just as much was how hard it
was to get back in. Fred had been unaware of how
many men and women his age and income level
were looking for the few high-paying jobs that
were vacant. He found he had to settle for some-

thing less just to get steady work, and to face having to sell his new home and to use his own corporate jargon, down size his budget.

Some time later Fred opened up to an old college friend and told him all his troubles. Near the end of the confession, he suddenly said something he had not fully realized before. "It's funny," Fred commented. "With all these problems and losses, I've found two gains. I've spent more time with my wife and family than I ever did all the years I was jetting around the country. I've also had time to go back to my church."

Not always but often there is a compensation that shows how a problem leads to an opportunity. When St. Paul reflected on his poverty, imprisonment and suffering in a Roman prison, he too recognized the law of compensations. To the church in the colonial city of Philippi he wrote that to preach the gospel in the face of adversity, he had suffered the loss of everything he had. But he added it was like losing "useless rubbish" compared to what he had gained (Philippians 3:8, J.B.Phillips).

Turning reversal into renewal is the challenge every sufferer meets. St. Paul could easily have thought his mission had come to a dismal, disappointing end with his arrest. How could he preach the gospel from a prison cell? St. Paul found a way. He could preach it to his guards. He could give them good news about a liberation they needed even though he was the one in chains. He could also write letters to his churches and to his colleagues, letters that have inspired people ever since as "the prison epistles." St. Paul was not stopped as a missionary by being shut up. He turned his problem into an opportunity.

Isn't that what Nelson Mandela did in South Africa all the years he was behind bars there? He was only partly a prisoner. He became also a symbol. Others spoke his message outside but no one spoke as loudly as he did inside. Free at last he is now a world figure. But would he be if he had not been imprisoned, if instead he had been just another one of the many who struggled against apartheid? What was intended to break Mandela made him. The law of compensations worked.

The list is endless. Canada's ambassador to Australia does not walk around in striped pants. He does not walk around at all because Rick Hanson is a paraplegic. As a young athlete who lost the use of his legs, Rick could understandably have become preoccupied with his handicap, drunk deeply from the cup of self-pity, and generally have wondered why God or fate had done him in. Instead he developed powerful shoulders and arms by compensating exercises until he was strong enough to travel by wheelchair all around the world. The object of his Herculean effort was to raise money for medical research. That he did, but at the same time inspired a nation with an example of what anyone of us can do when life goes against us.

The years we have on earth are a series of compensations. I miss my four children and the times we had as a family, the years of Sunday night dinners when my wife fed roast beef to a series of boy and girlfriends that gave us a big table both she and I enjoyed to the full. But their growing up has not meant the "empty nest" I read about. It has meant filling up our lives with other joys and satisfactions. We have found the reversal of a home of six to a home of two can also be a renewal for the two. When their children are grown, a husband and wife can renew their own relationship. In their loss they can gain a compensation.

My wife's own career path has shown the law of compensations at work. When our youngest child reached elementary school, Margaret became a student herself by enrolling in the evening division of our university. After several years of part-time study and one full-time year she took her degree at a convocation happily attended by a very proud husband and four children. Next she qualified as a school teacher herself, and a few years later entered the highly competitive world of real estate. Not only were all four children gone but her husband was in the nation's capitol most of the week as a Member of Parliament. What better way of compensating than doing something she had had to postpone because of other priorities?

Life brings us all some losses. Through marriage breakdown or bereavement we lose our spouses or they lose us. Through aging we lose our appearance, our strength, our fitness. Perhaps we lose some of the security we had taken for granted through financial crises we cannot control. We lose our friends and colleagues, the work we loved so much and the achievements we prized. Life's like that. It is a series of losses. But often they can be turned into gains. A person who believes that is on the way to recovery from any setback that life can bring.

How can you and I believe when we live in a world like this? We'll live a lot happier and do a lot better if we believe in the law of compensations. Few bereaved people have felt the loss of a spouse more than Dorothy. She became almost neurotic, unable to share her grief with her friends, turned dangerously in on herself, unwilling to give even an iota of herself to anyone else. At last she chanced to meet an old friend who had been married for years to one of Dorothy's roommates at college. He was a widower, and fortunately for Dorothy, one who was determined to share his life again with someone. He was so cheerful, upbeat, and fun-loving that Dorothy soon found that she could not help smiling when he came around. She even laughed at some of his jokes. Soon she found herself living again because she was giving again. Life brings its reversals, but they can be changed into renewals.

No one who likes politics accepts a defeat easily, but it too has compensations. I'd rather be in than be out, but it's easier being out. Gone are the incessant pressures, the constant mobility, the relentless hectoring, the personal vulnerability. But much more important than what has gone is what has come. There is a life after political death. It is a life with time to enjoy my marriage again. It gives me time for the theological issues to which I have given most of my life. Especially it gives me the chance to write and rewrite this book. It would not have happened if the 1988 election had gone as it should.

Probably that was why Henry Wadsworth Longfellow, another New England source of wisdom, wrote in the poem "Resignation:"

"...often celestial benedictions
Assume this dark disguise."

They come "disguised" because we would not recognize the compensations if they did not bring us problems before they showed us opportunities.

If what has gone from your life cannot be changed, you can be when you accept the law of compensations. Give up dwelling on what you have lost and search for what you can find.

The Law of
Prospects

Some people become bigger because of suffering they have endured. Some become smaller. Obeying the law of compensations is not the only thing that makes a difference. Believing in the law of prospects is another.

I learned this law when I was a young minister trying to build a church. I had started with a small membership, a vacant lot, and a sign that said a church would be built on that lot. The first years were not easy and I could have become discouraged if I had not learned about the law of prospects from some of my parishioners. Many were salespersons — steel, cars, real estate, insurance, suits — and from them I learned that building a congregation was something like making sales. Both began with believing there were prospects. No matter how many polite refusals I got, I had to realize each call I made was a new call. Each represented a prospect, and if I made enough of them I would add to the church. It proved true. On my first Easter I had twenty-two people at church. Ten years later there were over nine hundred.

During those first years I learned something about psychological suffering, about how frustration and failure feel, especially when you are trying your hardest. But I became a better minister and a better person through learning to believe I had prospects as well as problems. As a minister I learned that behind every door there is a potential parishioner. As a professor I have learned that within every student there is a prospective success. As a person I know that in every problem there is a possible opportunity.

Whatever be the suffering, it can contribute to character building when a person invokes this law of prospects. History is filled with examples of men and women who saw possibilities where lesser people saw only obstacles. Robert Bruce, king of the Scots in the fourteenth century, despaired of resisting the stronger forces of England in their persistent determination to subject Scotland. He had lost to them in battle and had had to flee to an island refuge off the coast of his rugged land. He thought he had no prospects until he filled his solitude one day by watching the efforts of what Winston Churchill has called "the most celebrated spider known to history." What intrigued the Bruce — as the Scots called him — was the spider's determination to build a web in spite of repeatedly failing to make the necessary leap from one rock to another. At last the spider did leap the span and established the first line of its web. Then another and another until the web was secured. Robert Bruce resolved he would be as dauntless as the spider. He returned to the mainland, rallied his forces, had himself declared king at Scone, and defeated the English army sent against him.

A Hollywood ending? It did not have to end that way at all. Robert Bruce could have stayed on that island and spent the rest of his days securely feeling sorry for himself. Some of us do that when life goes against us the way it had for him. Instead he turned suffering into learning when he discovered the law of prospects.

North America is what it is because that Scottish king has had many successors. This continent is the

result of men and women, great and ordinary, coming here to prospect for a better life. The
Stackhouse family was typical. Three of my ancestors joined William Penn on the *Welcome* to sail
from England and seek a new life in the Penn
colony, later called Pennsylvania. They were
Quakers. Like many others in the persecuted
Society of Friends, they had discovered that neither
relatives nor community wanted them around. It
could have made them paranoid or it could have
made them conform. Instead it made them look for
other prospects.

That's the first option we have to look at when
trouble comes. Most of the world's progress has
evolved that way. It has come from men and
women recognizing difficulties have to be suffered
but do not have to be endured. In spite of repeated
failures in his experiments, Alexander Graham Bell
kept trying until he succeeded in inventing the telephone. Marie Curie displayed the same formula of
vision plus perseverance when she and her husband labored for years to give us the benefit of
radium. Franklin D. Roosevelt changed his country
and the world by refusing to believe a person in a
wheelchair could not be president of the United
States. When many people saw only the reversal of
an empire, Margaret Thatcher saw prospects for the
renewal of a nation. Character is built through chál-
lenge when prospects are recognized.

That's certainly what the Bible teaches, especially
by the example of the people who populate its

pages. Let's look at one. Moses is a prophet to three faiths — Judaism, Christianity and Islam. Millenia after he lived, his name is honored by two billion adherents to those religions. No matter how we measure greatness, Moses has to qualify. Yet he knew years of failure, rejection, alienation. His success did not even begin until he was middle-aged. In spite of that, Moses grew with his difficulties. One reason was that he never lost respect for the law of prospects. He kept believing problems could become opportunities.

Read his story in the second book of the Old Testament, the book called Exodus, because it tells the story of Moses leading his people out of Egypt towards the land the lord God promised them. It was not easy. But it was inspiring. Just think of keeping a nation of migrant refugees together, feeding and providing for them in a desert, organizing them into a fighting force, and preparing them to found a country. Moses did it. No matter how rebellious, divisive, and self-pitying his people became, Moses never took his eyes off the prospects that had led them out of Egypt. Even when there seemed no hope he found prospects. When their food supplies ran out, Moses learned the desert could supply its own bread. When his people cried for water, he showed how water could spring from a rock. Lesser people cringed before the challenge of the day. He lifted them above it with prospects of the future.

In an essay called "Prospects," Emerson wrote

that "the invariable mark of wisdom is to see the miraculous in the common." You and I are surrounded by the commonplace every day. But it can show us prospects too, if we look for them.

John Burns, a pioneer of the British Labor Party, said the worst attribute of the poor was the poverty of their desires. It's true of many. But not of all. One reason Canada became a the second largest country in the world was a leader who had landed on its shores as a Scottish immigrant boy, the son of a stone mason. From the day he sailed up the St. Lawrence with scarcely a penny in his pocket until he became the first prime minister of a new nation, John A. Macdonald had to believe in prospects. When he started, he had nothing else. Poverty can be a roadblock. It can also be a launching pad.

That's why some of us may need the advice of Sophie Tucker. The "last of the red hot mamas" said: "I've been rich and I've been poor. Believe me. Rich is better."

That does not mean just being rich in money. There are other riches — knowledge, health, friends, family, skill, respect, peace. We can be poor in those ways too. Or we can be rich. We do not have to be beaten by life if we see we always have prospects.

Most historians respect Abraham Lincoln as the greatest of all the presidents of the United States. Yet he achieved this greatness only after years of mediocrity. His few years in the Congress were notable chiefly for being unnoteworthy. He was refused the only government appointment he ever sought. But Lincoln would not have become president if he had not undergone the disappointments that sent him back to Illinois. He had to go back there to develop himself as the moral leader of his state and his country in the face of the slavery crisis. If Lincoln had indulged himself with cynicism or pity, he would have been just another circuit-riding country lawyer. Abraham Lincoln had to recognize his prospects before he could become President Lincoln.

That's true of you and me. We know about our disappointments. We need to be just as clear about our prospects. Go into any community, perhaps your own. Ask who are the people who do the most to make it a better place to live. They are not always the best off. Often they are people with sickness in the home, or limited income, or personal struggles. But they are all believers. They believe their community has what it takes to be a better place. They also believe they have something to offer it. Not for them the incessant whining about the politicians and the system. They are too busy turning problems into opportunities.

I like that story about two boys, one rich, one poor. The rich boy had been given a pony by his indulgent parents. But he was was soon found crying outside the stable instead of enjoying his gift. When asked what was wrong, he explained that the pony was so beautiful, he was sure it would be stolen. The poor boy, however, was found in the stable digging in the manure as hard as his young arms could work his shovel. As he labored away he was laughing and singing. When asked, "Why?" he answered: "I figure it this way. With all this manure in here, there's got to be another pony down there somewhere!"

He had prospects. So do you and I. And they can make us bigger than our problems.

*When a Cross
Can Become a Plus*

Jesus taught people that persons who lose themselves can become persons who discover themselves (Luke 9:23-25). If we obey the law of compensations and the law of prospects, anyone of us can become that kind of person. We won't just suffer. We will become better people.

CHAPTER FIVE

Is This World a Fair Place if One Has to Pay the Price For Everyone Else?

Every November 11, I have the same mental vision. It's of miles and miles of white crosses stretching as far as the eye can see across every continent and island. Each cross marks the grave of someone who fell in war. There are so many — millions when they are put together — that they speak as nothing else can about "Man's inhumanity to man." But they speak about something else too. Something better. It is called vicarious sacrifice.

The term means that noblest of all human virtues, willingness to offer oneself for others. Since ancient times it has inspired men and women to deeds of sacrifice in war and peace. Its root is the Latin word *vicarius*, which means a substitute who can stand in for someone else. Our word vice has the same root and so we speak of a vice-chair as the officer who can stand in for the chair if he or she is absent. Vicariousness runs through the Bible. You may remember how Job offered sacrifices every day for his children at the family altar. They had committed the sins but their father was ready to pay the price for them. In the Book of Isaiah there are dramatic descriptions of a servant who suffers beating, imprisonment and finally death so that his people can be blessed (Isaiah 53:3-9). In the New Testament the apostles understood Jesus as one who had fulfilled this prophecy. For them Jesus was this suffering servant and his cross was his way of paying the price for every one else's salvation (I Peter 2:24-25).

Like many other spiritual traditions, Judaism and Christianity have thus taught people to believe a person can do nothing finer than sacrifice himself or herself for others. Loss of human life is a tragedy, but often it is also the tragic way that humanity is blessed.

That's why November 11 — as Remembrance Day in Canada, Veterans' Day in the United States — reminds us about what should not happen and reminds us about what should. This world is a place of evil where men and women are cut down by savage fire in battle. It is also a place of inspiration where men and women rise above every self-interest, including their own lives, to help save others.

If we wonder how we can possibly believe when this world is filled with the fury and rage of war, let's remember there is this other side too. The world is a worse place because war can make it into a hell. But it is also a better place because of all those who, like Jesus, have been ready to pay the price for everyone else.

Better
Together

First let's see what can make sense out of believing that no one can show greater love for humanity than to give one's own life for others.

In my teens I worked with another youth I will call Jeff. He was just another school dropout and in ordinary times might have drifted through life almost like a piece of scrap drifting down the stream. Many people do. But World War II was not an ordinary time, and Jeff began to do extraordinary things. Or so they seemed in our parochial lives. When he showed up one day in an air force uniform, he looked almost an adventurer. That is what he soon would be. As a gunner aboard a bomber plane, he shot down so many enemy planes he was soon commissioned an officer and later decorated. At the end of a successful tour of duty Jeff could have become an instructor. But he elected a second tour of bombing missions over Europe. This time Jeff was not as fortunate. On his third mission his plane was destroyed and the crew lost.

When news of his death came home, some friends commented on how foolish he had been to take the second tour. Maybe he was a fool. A venturesome one, a patriotic one, but still a fool. That is, unless a belief in vicarious suffering can dignify Jeff's death — and with it his life — as one person's gift to the human race. When I later sat in Parliament I often thought of him and all the other Jeff's and Jane's whose readiness to give themselves made democracy possible for those who came after them. If they had not been ready to face the most evil alliance of primitive brutishness and modern power the world has ever seen, where would humanity be now? The eighties ended with an explosion of freedom in the countries behind the Iron Curtain. Would it have been possible but for the few who, during the long years of Communist repression, kept the light of freedom at least flickering. Would the many now be entering democracy's halls if the few had not been ready to suffer exile, imprisonment, torture, even death?

Only a belief in vicarious suffering can dignify the sacrifice of Jeff and millions of others since his death. That is why their survivors cling to this belief. It is hard enough to accept the death of a loved one, but so much harder to believe it was for nothing. If people believe their country and their world are just a great cosmic self-serve center, personal sacrifice is the most pathetic self-deception we can conceive.

But what if vicarious suffering is right? Then being human is different. Speaking of corporate membership makes sense. Corporate comes from the Latin word *corpus*, for body. Member means being part of something, and we speak of our legs and arms as being members of our bodies. If one of them is amputated, we speak of it as being dis-membered, no longer a part.

Vicarious suffering makes sense only if that is what being human involves. We have to understand ourselves as different from the kind of person described in one of Bob Dylan's insightful songs:

How does it feel
To be without a home
There's no direction home
Like a complete unknown
Just like a rollin' stone.[1]

Unlike a rolling stone, a human being has to have relationships to make life complete. But those rela-tionships can mean a readiness to suffer vicariously for others. It can mean offering one's life in war. It can mean serving others in peace. It can mean a young nurse I met in an Ethiopian village where she had gone after being raised in an Ontario town.

[1]Like A Rolling Stone. Words and music by Bob Dylan. Copyright 1965 by M. Whitmark & Sons, 1970 by Warner Bros. Inc. Page 42. Bob Dylan Self-Portrait. Published by Bob Dylan Words Music Company Inc.

Or it can mean a Salvation Army couple I met in Central America. After years of retailing in a Canadian city, they were using their retirement to help people with alcohol problems. Whether it is losing one's life in a single dramatic act of sacrifice or giving it in years of patient, daily service the meaning is the same. One is paying the price for others.

What makes sense out of this is believing we share a common humanity that makes us members one of another. Being human means more than rolling through life like a stone going downhill. It means belonging to others and being ready to give oneself for them.

That is why the cross of Jesus continues to be worn by men and women all over the world. It reminds them and others of what is so easy to forget, especially in the west of today.

The Me Culture

Vicariousness can seem like a word from a foreign language in today's culture. It has become so self-centered that Tom Wolfe's descriptive phrase, the Me Generation, immediately tells us what we have become. We do not need an explanation. It is every man for herself!

In this culture, individuality is all that counts. Membership is not real. One is never really a part of anyone else. We do not form organic unions with other people because that implies we belong to each other. Instead we now talk of coalitions because they can be dissolved as easily as they can be arranged.

In the Me Culture nothing and no one is allowed to have priority over the individual. A husband or wife is entitled to walk away from a marriage when it interferes with the personal priorities of either partner. Marriage has been redefined. It is not a union that can be dissolved only with great difficulty when it is clear no good option remains. It has become a partnership that can be terminated when either person wishes.

In this Me Culture the same absence of meaningful relationships is found everywhere. A company can take for granted its right to shed employees as if they were expendable assets. On the other side of the bargaining table, being loyal to the firm seems absurd. In today's democracies government has become a balancing act between one self-interest and another. Elections are won by those who persuade the majority they offer the most.

If the Me Culture is right, then Jeff and millions of others were wrong. So is the young Britisher I met when I visited the Third World orphanage he was administering. So is the brilliant Toronto surgeon friend who has given his life to develop new operations that enable people to walk again. Why should entertainers put on benefit concerts if they aren't paid for it? Why should anyone volunteer to do anything? Vicariousness has no place in a Me Culture.

The Now
Culture

Turn that way of life over. On its flip side you will find what I will call the Now Culture. People consumed with themselves live only in the present. They show little interest in the past and feel no obligation to the future. Instead of having a way of life, they have what they call a life-style. The term is appropriate because nothing is as transient as a style, nothing so out of date as yesterday's fashion. Just as the Me Culture concentrates on the individual, the Now Culture focuses on that individual's generation. Whether it is the Now of the singles bar or the Now of the senior citizen's home, the presupposition is the same. Life revolves around the present so much that one generation has no contact with another one that can be avoided. Many young people do not know their grandparents, and few know anything about their families beyond that third generation. In a time of almost perfect contraception, spouses can choose to live without children at all. Effectively cut off from their parents, they can live in a one-generation world.

That was not how Isaiah's suffering servant saw life. He was called to suffer because of a previous generation's sins, and his vocation included obtaining salvation for people still to be born. He belonged to a multi-generational culture.

Should it be out of date? The ecology crisis of the nineties shows it is as current as the news of the latest disaster. We are only partially responsible for the world's present danger. Much of the pollution was decided by those who ran the world before us. But that does not let us off the hook. We are handing on to the future a world we have made worse than the one we received. The sins of the fathers are being visited on their children and grandchildren — just as the Bible warned they would be. What future can there be if being human does not include belonging to others?

Civilization has to be a succession of interlocking generations, each one intertwining with those who have gone before and those who have yet to come. All of us are trustees for this world. We do not own it any more than we created it. We do have to look after it, if possible handing it on to our successors in better shape than it had been in when we came along.

Vicarious sacrifice means that each generation should look after the well-being of those yet to come. A casual look around your own community can show what I mean. Imagine yourself taking a child to your community hospital for an anti-polio injection. Think of the men and women who organized, recruited, solicited, and donated so that the hospital could be built. Ask yourself what the hospital could do for that child without the vaccine

Jonas Salk and other researchers developed after years of painstaking effort. Or what would have happened to low income children if Dr. Salk had patented his vaccine and sold it for profit?

Each generation stands on the shoulders of those who have gone before and now provide support. Each one is called to take its turn at providing another set of shoulders. That can mean vicarious suffering. It may be the sacrifice of a soldier in a UN peacekeeping mission or a research scientist in a laboratory. It can mean something as ordinary as parents bringing their pay home — or giving up vacations to finance their children's education.

Vicarious suffering is not outdated. Our times, like all those before them, show the Me Generation should be replaced by a We Culture, one that provides for the future, even as it has received from the past.

*The
Down Side*

Admirable as vicarious suffering is, it can be used to cover up needless pain inflicted on people. An indefensible waste of life can be excused by claiming it was a necessary sacrifice.

That's the message I took from an unforgettable Sunday morning walk with my son, then ten years old, and one of his pals across a Pennsylvania field where General George Edward Pickett led his disastrous charge in the Battle of Gettysburg.

I wanted to see how it felt that late afternoon in 1863 when 15,000 gray-coated youths, filled with hope and misplaced faith, obeyed the unbelievable order to march. It was such madness that the corps commander could not speak when General Pickett asked if he should begin the charge his men had been standing in line all day to make. General James Longstreet had disagreed with his commander-in-chief, the renowned Robert E. Lee. He could not bring himself to answer Pickett, it is reported, beyond nodding his head. As more than a century later the three of us walked across the same field, I could see why. It was an order to commit suicide.

Line on line fell as it marched, colors flying, drums rolling. Two out of every three Southern soldiers under the relentless fire of artillery and riflemen massed on Cemetery Hill. What started out to be a battlefield was soon a graveyard. When the survivors finally straggled back to their lines, General Lee rode among them confessing, "It was all my fault."

In a way, it was. But not all his fault. The slaughter was not due to one general, but to all the political and military leaders who initiated a war that could have been avoided, and continued it when it could have been halted.

I might reluctantly see the point of this spectacle of mass sacrifice if it had taught us something in the years since. But names such as Gallipoli, the Somme, Dieppe, Vietnam show we have not learned much about human wastage. The same tragic story can be told and retold because governments, generals and people excuse their callousness by claiming the fallen died necessary deaths for their country, or democracy, or some other cause higher than themselves. Too often the real explanation is they died because authorities were wrong when they planned strategies or organized supplies or declared war. I have become convinced the world would be a more peaceful place if all the fighting had to be done by people over fifty. It is too easy to pour out the rich red wine of youth.

The abuse of this human willingness to make sacrifices is not confined to war. It shows up in personal relationships and corporate policies in peacetime, too. Children can take advantage of their parents readiness to deny themselves. Mothers and fathers can be just as adept at manipulating a child's love to serve the parents' self-interest. At work employers appeal to staff to deny themselves for the company or the public. But those same owners may sell that company without a single thought of how the sale will affect the workers who helped make it a success.

One
for All

Jesus said the greatest love humans can give is shown when we are ready to lay our lives down for

others (John 15:13). That he was right has been con-
firmed in every age since. The story of civilization
has been written in red by all the men and women
who have given themselves to lift the level of life
for others. The human race is like a rope with many
strands that are bound together to make it strong.

Yes, this belief can be abused. Tragically abused.
But it remains a truth on which all of us depend.
Often vicarious sacrifice is the only message that
can comfort the sorrow of losing loved ones. If
their sacrifice was not in vain but with a purpose,
those who are left to mourn can do it with courage.

That is why the November 11 ceremonies touch
the heart. It is why the Vietnam memorial at
Arlington Cemetery means so much to those who
go there searching for the name of a family member
or a friend. Their deaths are no less painful to recall.
But they gain a dignity when they are connected to
a cause they believed was worth dying for.

Judged by all the standards of fairness there are,
it is not fair to expect one person to pay the price for
everyone else. But sometimes there is no one else to
pay it.

CHAPTER SIX

Must Suffering and Death Have the Last Word?

It is claimed that all of us who remember the assassination of President John Kennedy can also remember exactly what we were doing that unforgettable afternoon of Friday, November 22, 1963. I can. It was as though the whole world watched one of the ugliest acts of history. One moment a vibrant leader was greeting his people. The next moment part of his head was blown by the assassin's bullet into the hands of his unbelieving wife.

I write of it now because it makes me ask how this world can be enough to do justice to human beings. A shining life becomes a helpless victim. A model of vigor is turned into a lifeless mass. If this world is all there is, it isn't enough.

A generation later it is even timelier to look beyond the world we can see. There is so much dying, so much suffering, so many young lives truncated, so many hopes stillborn. How can this world tell the entire human story?

Students are gunned down in Beijing's Tiananmen Square. Thousands of Ethiopians languish in political prisons. In northern Ireland, Roman Catholics and Protestants bomb and shoot one another. The Christians and Muslims of Lebanon turn a country into a graveyard. The Central American city of San Salvador swarms with homeless squatters driven into the capitol by a never-ending war. What a pathetic world this is if suffering and death have the last word in the human story.

It has always been so. Job wrestled with the same anguished dilemma. How can this life be enough when innocent people have to take what is put on them? When a person dies, Job asked, can that person live again? Can there be another chance, another life where the wrong can be made right, the crooked straight, the uneven level?

It was that kind of question that drove the leading intellect of the Age of Reason to look beyond reason and conclude justice demands we get a life beyond this one. A philosophy professor in East Prussia near the end of the eighteenth century, Immanuel Kant, reasoned there was not enough time in a person's short life span to obtain justice in this world. So many decent people were shafted and so many human devils given success, that Kant said there had to be a world where the score would be evened.

Otherwise, he argued, this world could not be thought subject to a divine sovereign. A just God could not allow such injustice to continue without judgment taking place somewhere, sometime.

I agree with Kant. This world cannot be all there is if God is just. To believe in a future life beyond this one is not easy. It demands we stretch our minds to their furthest limits even to grasp a faint image of a life beyond this one. But justice demands we make the effort. This world is not enough to give justice to all who deserve it.

I know I risk losing you if you are one of the many who turn off theology if it speaks about a future life. According to opinion polls almost everyone believes there is a God, but far fewer believe there is a life after death. Perhaps you don't. But stay with me. You may change your mind. Life after death cannot be proven nor disproven. But it can be believed, and those who believe it have something to help them cope with innocent suffering.

No Place Now
for Heaven

Since civilization began, people have held different beliefs about a future life. Primitive cultures reveal burial practices that showed people expected the dead to carry on just they way they had on earth. Centuries before Christ, Hindus thought people had not one but a series of incarnations on earth. Each was a reward or punishment for the previous one. Later Judaism and early Christianity believed in a final judgment when the dead would rise from their graves to face God.

In most developed countries now, fewer people think that way. We assume it means thinking the universe is like a three-storey structure. Heaven is the top one, hell the basement and earth is in between. Since few conceive the universe that way now, many assume belief in a future life must be jettisoned too.

Their problem is that they have become one-dimensional. I mean they can conceive only what they can know by their senses, or what can be contained within what they can see, touch, smell, hear or taste. Since we cannot know what is beyond this world by the senses, some of us assume it is not "for real." These people are one-dimensional.

It is not a new problem. Centuries before Christ, the Greek philosopher Plato said many men and women could not grasp anything that was not in front of their noses. He said they were like certain cave dwellers. In their cave these people, he said, were chained so that they could face only the cave's inner wall. From the light behind them, they could see reflections of other people walking past the cave's entrance. Since they had never been able to turn around and face these people, they thought these reflections were actually the people. What were shadows were taken for realities. Plato's message still applies. Many of us have become so chained by the assumptions of our culture, we think they are all the reality there is. We need a liberation to move beyond our one dimension.

How does a person make that move? It demands a choice. Belief in a future life is not a matter of proof or disproof. It is a matter of choice. The sceptic makes a choice just as the believer does. Neither knows. Each believes. One says there is a great big nothing after death. The other hopes for something.

When I called on two men who had just lost their wife and mother, a visiting friend commented. "Now she knows. The rest of us are just guessing." Three hundred years earlier one of the liveliest minds of Europe, Blaise Pascal, made the same point in his famous "Wager Argument" for the existence of God. This brilliant mathematician cum inventor cum philosopher urged people to bet their lives on God. If we do, Pascal reasoned, we may find an eternity of happiness when death comes. But if our belief turns out to be a mistake, we will have lost nothing. We will have had the comfort of our faith through this life and we would have had to die anyway. On the other hand if we deny this belief and it turns out to be true, we will miss our chance.

Pascal's argument sounds crass. But it is more profound than crass. Our ultimate destiny is beyond affirming or denying through proofs or arguments. Each person must choose what to believe. The choices we have now are the same that Pascal had and that Plato had. They have nothing to do with being modern. They have everything to do with being human. Our world view has changed, but our human need has not.

I learned that truth one Saturday evening when summoned to the home of a couple whose thirty-year-old son had just been killed in an accident. The shock was so great that his mother and his young widow were both under sedation when I arrived. But the father was waiting for me. It is never easy to meet a family struck by tragedy. But I expected to find this one especially difficult because I had little rapport with these people. They were not hostile, just distant. But as so often happens, need provided the bond. I shared a few words with the father. I spoke about our belief in eternal life. It sounded like good news to him. With tears in his usually cold eyes he clutched my hand and said, "There has to be something."

Why there has to be something cannot be explained by science. Nor can it be explained away. It is not a matter for reason either. It is a matter of a person's finding what meets our human need. If someone finds another way to meet that need, so be it. But in this age of computers as much as in the age of counting beads, this belief helps many face life's greatest challenge.

In the tin mines of north Africa during the Roman empire, the manual work was done by slaves brought from all over the empire. They rowed themselves across the sea in galley ships, driven by the lash. They were marched across the desert and then driven underground, never to see the light of day again. Archaeologists have since discovered words and pictures drawn on the walls of these slaves' subterranean prisons. One word has been found repeated more than any other. It is the word Life. In the midst of this death on earth, they believed in life. Many of them were Christians and the good news for them was Jesus' promise that, as he had risen from the dead, so would they.

Should we feel a condescending pity for these poor wretches who consoled themselves with a belief sophisticated men and women do not need any longer? It depends on us. In the prison camps of Nazi Germany, Christian prisoners gathered clandestinely to hear the gospel and receive Holy Communion if one of the prisoners was a pastor. Often they were joined by others who were not practising Christians. It is said that regardless of faith they could all identify with Jesus when the story of his passion was read. They saw he was once just as they had become — human beings about to die. They could hope that they could become just what he was — a person raised from the dead.

There is nothing modern about dying. There is nothing out of date about believing.

Not Pie
in the Sky

For some people the problem is not believing a future life is possible. In the face of this world's injustices they cannot see its relevance. For them it means pie in the sky, by and by. What they want is bread on earth right now.

I have a lot of empathy with this objection. Religious people have always found it easy to be diverted from social challenge. Two centuries ago, William Wilberforce persuaded the British Parliament to abolish slave trade throughout the British Empire. But for some reason he did not see the need for wage slaves in his own country to be liberated. As much as by the Industrial Revolution's new machinery, Britain's economic progress was made possible by the men, women and children who dragged themselves through lives of drudgery. But Wilberforce was blind to their plight. In one of his writings he observed that the poor had a spiritual advantage over the rich because they were not beset by as many temptations. So they had a better chance to make it to heaven.

Wilberforce was not alone in thinking that way, and Karl Marx was not all wrong in claiming religion was the opiate of the people. It was — in the hands of churches that taught the masses to be content with the state to which God seemed to have called them.

But that was not the only Christian message heard. Men such as Thomas Arnold, Lord Shaftesbury and Frederick Maurice gave people another way of understanding their faith. It would be called the social gospel because it offered good news about social justice.

I write about them because they showed how people could believe in God and heaven without losing interest in this world. The same is true today. All over the world the call to justice is made by people who also go to church, offer worship, say prayers, and believe in a future life. Serving humanity on earth does not mean losing faith in God in heaven.

The two go together. Each meets a human need. Those who think social justice is everything forget it cannot deal with every challenge men and women face. No amount of medicare, public housing, educational opportunity, fairness in the work place can deal with those needs and anxieties that are inside us all. Will more generous funding of community agencies make sure no man will abuse his wife or his children? If our inner city ghettos are transformed into picture book suburbs, will there be no marriage breakdowns, no family desertions, no twisted personalities? No matter how much we improve our social policies, human problems will still face us. Medical care can extend life expectancy but death will still be waiting a little further down the road. This world — and its governments — cannot provide for all our needs.

So believing in a future life should not be discarded as irrelevant. No one could have been more involved in this world than the man who many still see as the greatest leader the United Nations has ever had. Yet Dag Hammarskjöld could hold such an other-worldly view as this one he expressed in *Markings*:

> In the last analysis it is our conception of death which decides our answer to all the questions that life puts to us...

Belief in a future life is not irrelevant to the way we live here and now. It is as basic as putting on each person the high value that person deserves.

Everyone
Counts

When you believe in heaven, you also believe everyone counts on earth. To appreciate that, let's think about Jim, that young arthritic I wrote about in Chapter Four. Picture him being lowered into his grave after his final release from this life. The only fragile thread connecting his short, pain-filled life to goodness and reason is that it's over. But that is not much to say about a human being. Can it be enough? The same could be said for a dead animal.

So let's say about Jim what St. Paul says in his First Epistle to the Corinthians. We can say Jim is going to be raised from the dead to a life such as he did not know on earth. This new life will not just continue the crippling disease he suffered on earth. He will be given a new body. We do not have to remember just the Jim we knew. We can picture the Jim he is to become.

Is this fantasy? Or is it a symbol? It can be a way of saying Jim's death is not the final out in a game he has already lost. It is the beginning of something better than he has ever known. His arthritic body is the one we bury — it is not the one he will have in the resurrection. So we can picture him with a new dignity that he lacked all those years in his sick bed. His body is no longer the wreck that it was when laid in the ground.

If that seems a flight from reality, I ask you to consider you might be flying that way too. When I go to funeral homes I am impressed at the effort made to disguise the reality of death. No one there speaks of people being dead. They have passed on. Visitors are not shown something admitted to be a dead body. They are shown what looks like a sleeping person in what is called a slumber room. There we find quiet background music. Everyone speaks in hushed tones. The whole atmosphere suggests no one has really died at all.

So where do we get this notion that it is religion that is flying from reality? Even worse is the current preference of some families to have no observance at all. There is no visiting, no service, no committal, nothing but what the law requires for the disposal of a dead body. It is like a game of let's pretend — let's pretend this person never lived at all.

The genuine realists are those who take death seriously. They acknowledge the person has really died. They also affirm this person still counts. The physical remains might be as useless now as a deflated balloon, but that body is not the whole person. When Jim was buried, his parents, a few relatives and his parish priest testified Jim was much more than a lifeless mass to be put in the ground. He was someone who still counted.

If any age of history needs to see that, ours does. Think of how little the ordinary people of our world count for. Along with hundreds of others they push their way into a subway car to go to work each morning. Jostled from one station level to another before entering the high-rise office tower for the day, they seem like worker bees going back to the hive of commerce. Can they see themselves as counting for anything more?

Yes, they can if they believe they are known in heaven and there is a place for them there. They are not just bytes on a global computer. Their names stand for people of value in the sight of God himself.

That value does not begin just after death, either. Just as no one can die in my place, no one else can live in my life. The fact that I must die my death also means I must live my life. So asserted Martin Heidegger, perhaps the most significant existentialist philosopher of this century.

What we believe about dying is thus basic to what

we think about living. To believe that I will enter eternity as a person with a name known to God is to believe I can live on earth as an individual with an identity that is mine alone.

That is not another way of expressing the Me Culture. Just the opposite. If I believe that about myself, I find it easier to believe it about other people. They too have individual worth just as I do. They too can live their own lives as I must live mine.

Judged by the values of the Me Culture, Jim was not really worth bothering about. He had no productivity. He added nothing to the GNP. He tied down two parents who could have done something more useful for themselves and society.

But judged by a belief in a future life, Jim counted for a lot just because he was a human being with an eternal destiny. To look at him in his sickbed was to be consumed by the sight of a crippled body. But to see him as a person was to believe in a young man with the same everlasting future as anyone else.

I want to believe that for not only Jim but for every other sufferer on this earth. I want to believe it for my father whose deathbed I sat beside for five nights while he fought for breath. I want to believe it for my mother who died a tiny fraction of the woman she had been in her good years. I want it for my oldest brother who died after years of outward suffering and inward struggle. I want it for my other brother whose years of physical deprivation should give him a chance for a better life than he has had in this world. I want it for my wife's father whose last months on earth were such a torture for him. I want it for all those who have had to wrestle with sickness only to be flattened by it before being carried from this life.

I also want it for you and me. "Everyone wants to go to heaven, but no one wants to die" is a saying coined for people like me. I like it here. Like the men and women in ancient Greek mythology I love this world. I love the sunshine and the sky, the trees and the water in the northern scene outside the study window where I am writing these words. Given my druthers I'd stay on earth another thousand years — at least. But I too must come to terms with reality. So must you.

Neither of us has to believe in a future life. It is a choice. It's possible for you and me to think this one is all there is. But given the choice I'd rather believe there is more to being human than lying under the ground. I like life and I choose to believe there is more for us after this one. I don't want suffering and death to have the last word.

CHAPTER SEVEN

How Can a Person Make it Through a World Like This Successfully?

I grew up during the Great Depression. The 1930s were years of disillusionment and frustration. As did most of our friends and neighbors, my family had to drink deeply from their bitter cup. The years were made worse for us because my father, then in his sixties, suffered a physical breakdown. Its effects were exacerbated by the way he lost confidence in himself and for the rest of his life assumed failure was the lot he had to accept.

Those years were probably harder for my mother. It was difficult enough to be married to a man seventeen years older than she was. But when he was suddenly out of work, at home all day, every day, and was referring to himself as an invalid, the strain escalated dramatically.

I now marvel that my parents did not throw in

the towel, split up, and farm us children out to foster homes. Others did. But I am sure the thought did not even occur to them. It would not have fitted their beliefs, and whatever else our home lacked, beliefs it had in plenty.

We were taught to believe in our family, in the political establishment (that meant the Crown and the British Empire) in a moral order (that meant no stealing, lying, boozing, whoring or gambling), in the church and its clergy, and most of all, in God who watched over us all.

Regardless of what was happening to her and her family, my mother was confident God would provide a solution. He would judge the wicked and vindicate the righteous. That the facts did not seem to verify this belief did not bother her at all. I now see why. She needed to believe that to keep herself intact.

The same was true of my father. His confidence in God was all the more impressive because he had so little in himself. His spirituality was quietly passionate. To hear him pray was to listen to someone who really believed he was speaking to someone else. If he had been as sure of himself as he was of God, life might have gone better for him. But if he had lacked the underpinnings of that faith, my father might have been laid flat by the blows life dealt him.

Their faith may well have been the chief reason we got through those years as well as we did. With what is now called a marginal income, my parents kept my two brothers and me in a six-room house, respectably dressed, and fed three meals every day. Most important of all for their three sons, they stayed with each other and with us.

Instead of falling apart when our circumstances periodically went from serious to critical to impossible, my mother took on new strength. When things were at their worst she was at her best. Faced with a new crisis she would become creatively resourceful, unflinchingly determined, inexhaustibly energetic. If a man came from City Hall to turn the water off, she would search the house for money, put fifty cents in hand, and talk him into going on his way. When a relative got into trouble she was off like a shot to look after whoever was sick, deserted, or just upset.

My parents' belief that a divine providence was ordering the world and their place in it was never challenged by facts that contradicted them. The thirties were a time when young men from our neighborhood rode freight trains looking for jobs nowhere to be found. Year by year the threat of war grew larger. But its approaching thunder gave no alarm. They were sure God — and they — would prevail.

Although they never used the term "mystery" to refer to God, I can see now that was how they understood him. They had never heard of St. Augustine of Hippo but they would have nodded in agreement if they had listened to him remind people that the wisdom of God was inscrutable and his ways past understanding. They would certainly have thought it irreverent to think God's way must be justified before he could be believed.

This was not because they were credulous people. In day-by-day dealings with others they were often soft-hearted. No panhandler ever knocked on our door in vain, regardless of how limited the larder was. But my parents were not soft-headed. Like the prophets of the Old Testament, they believed God's ways were not our ways and he was not to be judged by human standards. In his good time he would make everything clear, and until then he was simply to be believed.

From one standpoint their attitude may strike you as gullible. But from another you can see it as the bedrock on which to secure your life. Wasn't Job right to spurn the advice that he curse God because of the way he had been treated? Wasn't he right to declare that even should God slay him, yet he would still trust God? That kind of faith can be what you, or anyone, needs to get through a world like this successfully.

My parents' marriage illustrates it. It was not a storybook romance. There were many times of tension and conflict. But they clung together and were better for it than if they had come apart. In the end they actually became touchingly near to each other. But it would not have happened if they had not believed a marriage did not depend on everything going well.

Although they did not use the word "mystery" when they spoke of marriage, that was how they understood it. They knew there was something in marriage that went beyond the empirical evidence of love and hate. It meant sticking together regardless.

That was how they understood belief in God too. They did not insist he lay everything on the line for them before they were ready to accept him. This was not because they were unschooled, unsophisticated and unquestioning. Many of their relatives, friends and neighbors had no more education than they had and yet held no serious belief in God or anyone else. My parents' faith was the way they chose to understand life. They could have chosen another way. They took this one because it helped them to cope with life more than rejecting it would have. The important feature of their choice was not just that they made it but that it made them.

My parents were not simplistic when they believed without question, protest or challenge. Nor were they pragmatic. They understood — as many an academic does not — how life is not explicable by propositions, ideas and arguments. It is ultimately not explicable at all. It is a mystery, like the one who has created it. As a mystery it can only be accepted, not explained. Had they studied theology, they would have become erudite in what thinkers had said through the centuries, but they would not have penetrated the mystery any more deeply than those scholars.

As that is true of God, so it is of humanity. Part of the divine image humans share is this element of mystery that, in the words of Psalm 139, makes us "fearfully and wonderfully made." However simple an ordinary man or woman seems outwardly, that person has an inner dimension not known to others. What makes you and me human is just what Shakespeare has Hamlet tell Guildenstern when Hamlet finds he is being manipulated as though he were a musical instrument:

You would play upon me; you would seem to know my stops;
you would pluck out the heart of my mystery.
(Act III: Scene ii)

Hamlet is right. We can be probed, analyzed, averaged, typed, measured, assessed, evaluated, screened, reviewed, categorized, classified, codified. But when it has all been done, we will retain what Hamlet calls the heart of his mystery. So we can accept each other without understanding one another. So we can accept God.

This means we can accept the tragic side of life without explaining it. We can accept how some suffer when they don't deserve to, and others thrive when they haven't earned it. As we have seen in the previous chapters, there are partial explanations, and each one fits different circumstances. But none wraps the mystery up and takes it away. President John Kennedy, at a news conference, mused about this and how it challenges the head of a state as much as it does the humblest of its citizens. Why is it, he asked, that some men are drafted and others do not have their numbers drawn, some are sent overseas and others serve at home, some see combat right away and others never hear a shot fired, some are wounded and others do not suffer a scratch? All a president or a professor or anyone else can do is ask the question. There is no final, full explanation.

Were my mother and father wrong to live as people who did not need to fathom why evil and innocent suffering were part of their world? Of course not. It was better to live the way they did. They expected rain would fall on their picnics some summer days, plant layoffs would hit some loyal employees, epidemics would infect some good people, bullets would stop some heroes, bank failures would bankrupt some honest people, bombs would fall on some sleeping citizens.

Although they never knew the name Sören Kierkegaard, they would have agreed with his claim that to be human is to suffer. They were not masochists any more than he was. They just knew, as this Danish father of existentialism did, that there is no way of getting through this world without taking some blows on the chin as well as pats on the back.

Is that why every great spiritual tradition has taught people to see life that way? The youthful Gautama Buddha grew up behind the walls of his father's palace without ever seeing the suffering that lay outside the gate. One day the gate was left open and he ventured into a world he had never

seen. There he saw a crippled beggar for the first
time, and realized he could not know what life was
all about until he freed himself from the limits his
father had imposed. How could he mature without
knowing suffering? What could he offer humanity
if he did not teach people how to cope with it?

*Believe
But Work Too*

So my parents, like so many great and humble
before and since, believed in God and each other
even when they lived in a world like this. But that
faith did not motivate them to become passively
helpless in the face of their problems. Just the
opposite. They might believe as though everything
depended on God but they worked as though
everything depended on them.

Both came from backgrounds where survival
demanded that people fend for themselves and their
families. They never lost that commitment. An
immigrant to Canada from England, my mother
arrived already a widow with a child at the age of
nineteen. She had to look for work in a city where
some factories posted signs saying: "No English
Need Apply." Before anyone ever thought of day-
care, she had to find someone to look after her baby
while she earned a living for the two of them.

At the age of thirteen my father left the New
Brunswick farm his father and brothers had cleared

with axes, and went into the bush to work as a lumberjack. He worked later on ships, in coal yards, in foundries, in factories. He worked until his body gave out. There was no unemployment insurance, no retraining after a physical injury, nothing but heavy work that paid barely enough to keep a man and his dependants alive until the next pay.

They raised their children to believe we had to make our way. The belief in God they taught us actually strengthened our self-reliance. They taught us it was wrong to pray for something to be given to us. All we could ask was the strength needed to obtain it. It was wrong to pray for success at school, right to ask for health needed to study, learn and pass. My parents did not conceive of God as someone who should be expected to take our troubles away. He was one we could count on to help us cope with them.

The whole interlocking network of spirituality in which we were reared reinforced this concept of God and the view of life it inspired. The church services we attended, the sermons we heard, the hymns we sang, the prayers we offered, the texts we memorized all buttressed this understanding of what the world was all about. We did not learn to believe in God because the world was a wonderful place. We learned to believe because that faith could help us make our way in a world with shadows as well as sunshine.

Would my mother and father have been better

off if they had joined others in renouncing belief in God or humanity because of what was happening in the world? When he lectured on existentialism in post-World War II Paris, Jean-Paul Sartre urged his students not to waste time on questions about God or faith. He reasoned that none of the evil in this world would disappear if they concluded there was a God.

Sartre was only half right. It was just as true that none of the evil disappeared because they concluded God did not exist and faith was futile. My parents would not have had fewer sicknesses or made more money or stayed together longer or been prouder of their children if they had taken any of the options others were accepting. Life would have been just as hard on them, and they would have been less able to take the blows and come back swinging.

Can a person make it through the sufferings of this life successfully? It is a rare man or woman who does not know pain in body or soul. The humanity of Jesus is clear not just in his being born but in his dying and being buried. To be human is to suffer. But to be human is also to cope with it. Job's experience shows believing enables one to cope. Part of Jesus' message on the cross is hanging on.

If you know a better way of coping, so be it. I'm glad you have found it. But I have written this book to share a way I have found with anyone who is looking for one. By following it you will not avoid the valleys and enjoy only the uplands. But you will walk through them and their shadows with more certain feet and more confident spirits.

A friend told me the ending of this book "should sing." I like that because throughout history believers have shown they can sing through the troubled nights that danger puts upon us. Why? Because they are sure those dark nights aren't everything.

Emily Dickinson's poetry has always meant much to me, especially this plea from the heart. It was written over a century ago. You might have asked its question last night.

> Is there such a thing as morning,
> Will there really be a day?
> If I were as tall as mountains,
> Could I see as far as they?
> O some sailor, O some scholar,
> O some wise man from the skies,
> Please to tell a little pilgrim,
> Where the place called morning lies.

I have written this book to share my belief that any night we enter must lead us to "the place called morning." It is better to believe when we live in a world like this.

Acknowledgements

My thanks go to many people who have shared
with me in this book: my wife, Margaret, for her
unfailing encouragement; my journalist son, John,
for several recommendations that have made this a
better book; the librarians of Wycliffe College, especially Adrienne Taylor and Gayle Ford; and of the
University of Toronto; my faculty colleague, Dr.
Glen Taylor, for his bibliographical assistance with
the Book of Job; the publishers and editors of
HarperCollins Canada and HarperSanFrancisco,
especially David Colbert for seeing the possibilities
in a manuscript that just "came over the transom;"
and all the many friends who kept asking, "How's
the book going?"
Scriptural quotations have been given these des-
ignations: New King James Version, NKJ; Revised
Standard Version, RSV; J. B. Phillips, The New
Testament In Modern English. Those undesignated
are my own renderings.